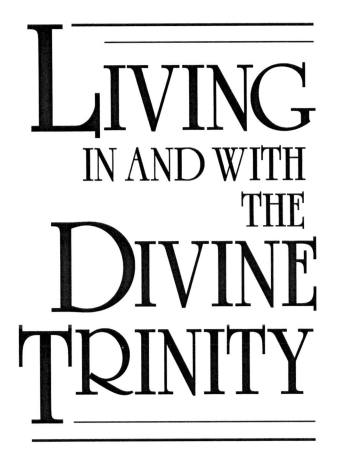

LIVING
IN AND WITH
THE
DIVINE
TRINITY

Witness Lee

Living Stream Ministry
Anaheim, California

First Edition, December 1990.

ISBN 978-0-87083-560-5

Published by

Living Stream Ministry
2431 W. La Palma Ave., Anaheim, CA 92801 U.S.A.
P. O. Box 2121, Anaheim, CA 92814 U.S.A.

Printed in the United States of America

17   18   19   20   21   /   9   8   7   6   5

CONTENTS

Title   *Page*

   Preface   5

1 The Vision concerning the Divine Trinity   7

2 The Vision concerning the Economy
    of the Divine Trinity   15

3 The Vision concerning the Dispensing
    of the Divine Trinity   23

4 Portions in the New Testament Revealing
    the Divine Trinity in the Divine Move
    and in Our Experience (1)   31

5 Portions in the New Testament Revealing
    the Divine Trinity in the Divine Move
    and in Our Experience (2)   41

6 Portions in the New Testament Revealing
    the Divine Trinity in the Divine Move
    and in Our Experience (3)   53

7 Portions in the New Testament Revealing
    the Divine Trinity in the Divine Move
    and in Our Experience (4)   65

8 Living in the Divine Trinity (1)   75

9 Living in the Divine Trinity (2)   83

10 Living with the Divine Trinity (1)   93

11 Living with the Divine Trinity (2)   101

12 Living with the Divine Trinity (3)   111

13 Living with the Divine Trinity (4)   121

PREFACE

This book is composed of messages given by Brother Witness Lee from February 22 to March 5, 1988 in a training in Irving, Texas.

CHAPTER ONE

THE VISION CONCERNING
THE DIVINE TRINITY

Scripture Reading: John 1:1; 17:24b; 1 Pet. 1:20; Heb. 9:14; Acts
2:23; Eph. 1:3-4; Gen. 1:1-2, 26-27; Col. 1:15; John 1:14; Gal.
4:4; Matt. 1:20; John 8:29; 16:32b; 14:10; Luke 4:1; Matt. 12:28;
1 John 1:7; Acts 20:28; 2:32; 10:40-41; Rom. 8:11; Acts 1:11;
1 Pet. 3:22; Phil. 2:9; Titus 3:4-6; Col. 1:12-13; 1 Tim. 1:15; John
3:5; Eph. 4:6; Gal. 2:20; John 14:17; 2 Cor. 13:14; Jude 20-21;
1 Cor. 12:28; Eph. 4:16; Acts 9:31; Eph. 4:4; Rev. 21:3, 9, 23;
22:17, 1-2

In this book we want to fellowship concerning the crucial
matter of our experience and growth in the divine life. As believers in Christ, we have such a marvelous, wonderful, excellent
life, the uncreated life of God Himself, the eternal life. But we
do not have much experience of this life, nor do we have the
adequate growth in this divine life. If we are going to experience
and grow in the divine life, we must be those who are living in
and with the Divine Trinity.

Even when we go to visit people, our burden is to bring the
Triune God to them and share with them the Triune God. In
Matthew 28:19 the Lord charged us to go and disciple all the
nations by baptizing them into the name of the Father and of
the Son and of the Holy Spirit, the very person of the Divine
Trinity. This is the purpose, the goal, and the aim of our going
out to visit people. We want to impart our Triune God as grace
and reality for salvation into the people we reach and bring the
people we reach into the reality of the Triune God.

We all need a vision concerning the experience of the Triune
God as our life. The Triune God in His trinity is for us to experience as our life so that we may grow in this life. The Divine

Trinity is absolutely wrapped up with the divine life. Actually, the divine life is the Divine Trinity. Apart from the Divine Trinity, there is no divine life. The divine life is a person, a three-one person. We must pay our full attention to the experience of the Divine Trinity as our life. Life is the Triune God.

The book of Ephesians reveals the church, and the church revealed in Ephesians is composed of and expresses the Triune God. The entire divine revelation in the book of Ephesians is constructed with and composed of the Divine Trinity (see the sixth paragraph of footnote 1 on 2 Corinthians 13:14, Recovery Version). We need to see a vision that governs and directs us. It is not sufficient for us to have mere doctrinal knowledge. We all need to see a divine vision concerning the Divine Trinity, in and with whom we need to live. In this chapter we want to see the vision concerning the Divine Trinity in eternity without beginning, in creation, in incarnation, in the living and work in Jesus' humanity, in His crucifixion, in His resurrection, in His ascension, in His salvation, in the Christian life, in the church life, and in eternity without ending.

IN ETERNITY WITHOUT BEGINNING

In the Beginning
the Son Being with the Triune God

Without the Divine Trinity there would not be eternity. The Divine Trinity is the composition of eternity. Eternity is the Triune God. Eternity comes out of and goes along with the eternal God. John 1:1 uses the phrase *in the beginning*. In the beginning the Word [the Son] was with [the Triune] God. *The beginning* in this verse refers to eternity past. In eternity was the eternal Word, the eternal Son of God, and this Word was with God. The Greek word for *with* in John 1:1 is *pros,* and here this word is a preposition of motion, implying living, acting, in union and communion with. This preposition implies fellowship. The Word not only was with God in eternity but also was fellowshipping and moving together with God. This shows us that in eternity past the Trinity was there in a very active way. *God* in John 1:1 refers to the Triune God, the Father, the Son, and the Spirit.

Handwritten top margin:
How do we know we're speaking from the Lord?
It requires actively seeking. fellowshipping with God. and sensing His love, and follow the sense
of love that we felt His love , speak. [John 5=19-20 Father loves us and, allow
we need to
Him to show us in cooperation [with Him (pray-read) → (revelation).]
what He is doing the way we can use to listen to messages

The Father Loving the Son
before the Foundation of the World

Handwritten right margin: Father loved the Son that love's ultimate goal is to be @my in the believe by love 2.

John 17:24b says that the Father loved the Son before the foundation of the world. This was before time began. In eternity the Father loved the Son. The loving One and the loved One are two yet one and are one yet two.

Handwritten: ~~Salvation is~~ God is motivated to speak through to ask the Son to do thing.

The Son Being Foreordained by the Triune God

In eternity without beginning, Christ [the Son] was foreordained by [the Triune] God (1 Pet. 1:20 and footnote, Recovery Version). He was prepared by God to be His redeeming Lamb (John 1:29) before the foundation of the world.

Handwritten right margin: Son's action Father's cooperate

The Spirit Being Eternal

The Spirit was also in eternity without beginning. Hebrews 9:14 speaks of the eternal Spirit. The eternal Spirit is of eternity, without any limit of time. He is the Spirit of all the ages. In eternity past when the Father and the Son were fellowshipping, when the Father loved the Son, and when the Son was foreordained by the Triune God, the Spirit was also there because He is the eternal Spirit, the Spirit of the ages.

Handwritten right margin: John 5:19-20

The Determined Counsel of the Triune God

Acts 2:23 says that Christ was delivered up by the determined counsel of [the Triune] God (see footnote 1 on verse 23, Recovery Version). Among the three of the Godhead, there was a council, and by this council a determined counsel was made. The Wuest translation of the New Testament says that Christ was delivered up by the counsel of God "in the council held by the Trinity." The determined counsel was made by the Triune God, who had held a divine council. The three-one God made a decision that the Son had to become a man and be crucified on the cross. The crucifixion of Christ was a fulfillment of God's determined counsel in eternity without beginning.

The Father Choosing Us in the Son
before the Foundation of the World

The Father of our Lord [the Son] chose us in Christ [the Son]

Make sure when you do a thing, you're in dispensing and for more dispensing.

10   LIVING IN AND WITH THE DIVINE TRINITY

before the foundation of the world (Eph. 1:3-4). The Father chose us, but He did it in Christ, the Son. He did not choose us directly. God the Father chose us in Christ as the element, the sphere, and the channel. Thus, in eternity past the Triune God was there fellowshipping, loving, foreordaining, working, and choosing.

IN CREATION

Genesis 1:1 reveals that [the Triune] God created the universe. The Hebrew word for *God* in this verse, *Elohim,* is plural in number. The subject *God* is plural, and the predicate *created* is singular. The plural God created the heavens and the earth. The three of the Godhead were creating; then Genesis 1:2 mentions the Spirit of God. It says that the Spirit of God was brooding upon the surface of the waters. The Triune God's Spirit was brooding upon the surface of the waters just like a hen brooding over its eggs.

The Triune God can also be seen in the creation of man. God said, "Let Us make man in Our [the Triune God's] image" (v. 26); so "God created man in His own [His Son's] image" (v. 27). God's own image is the Son's image. This is proved by Colossians 1:15, which tells us that Christ is the image of the invisible Triune God. Hebrews 1:3 says that the Son is the impress, the express image, of God's substance. Thus, we can see that the Divine Trinity was working in creation.

IN INCARNATION

The creation by God was for the old creation, but the incarnation is for the new creation. John 1:14 reveals that [the Triune] God became incarnated. The entire God—the Father, the Son, and the Spirit—was involved in the incarnation. This is also proved by other verses in the New Testament. Galatians 4:4 says, "God [the Father] sent forth His Son, born of a woman." God the Father took part in the incarnation. It was the Son's incarnation, but the Father sent the Son. In John 8:29 the Lord Jesus said, "He who sent Me is with Me." The Father sent the Son, and the Son said that the One who sent Him was with Him. Thus, the Son's incarnation is also the Father's incarnation. After sending the Son, the Father did not remain in the heavens. When the Son came in the womb of Mary, the Father was with the Son.

Matthew 1:20 says, "That which has been begotten in her is of the Holy Spirit." Jesus was begotten in Mary, and Jesus was of the Holy Spirit. These main verses show that the incarnation was not only of the Son but also of the Father and of the Spirit. All three of the Divine Trinity were incarnated. The birth of Jesus was with the Triune God. He was the complete God and the perfect man, the Triune God-man. He was the Triune God incarnated, the God who is the Father, the Son, and the Spirit. The incarnation was the incarnation of the Father, the Son, and the Spirit. The very Savior in whom we believe and whom we have received is the wonderful Triune God-man.

IN THE LIVING AND WORK IN JESUS' HUMANITY

The Triune God was in Jesus' living and work while He was on the earth. In John 8:29 the Lord Jesus said, "He [the Father] who sent Me [the Son] is with Me [the Son]." In the Son's living and work, the Father was with Him (16:32b). When the Son spoke, the Father did His works in the Son (14:10). Luke 4:1 tells us that Jesus [the Son], full of the Holy Spirit, was led by the Spirit. He was with the Father and full of the Spirit. In His living and in His work, the Spirit was with Him as well as the Father. Matthew 12:28 says that the Son cast out demons by the Spirit. The Son did not cast out demons without the Spirit, and He did not speak without the Father. When He spoke, the Father did His works. When He cast out demons, He did it by the Holy Spirit. The Divine Trinity was wrapped up with the living and work of Jesus while He was on this earth.

IN HIS CRUCIFIXION

The Divine Trinity can also be seen in the crucifixion of Jesus. First John 1:7 and Acts 20:28 show that the blood of Jesus [the Son] is considered as the blood of God [including the Father and the Son]. How could the very God have had blood? He had blood because He was mingled with a man. In God as the divine One alone, there is no blood. But in the man with whom He mingled Himself, there is blood. This God-man is one entity with two natures. In the divine nature there is no blood, but in the human nature there is blood; so the blood of Jesus is considered as the blood of God. Acts 20:28 says that

God obtained the church "through His own blood," and 1 John 1:7 refers to the blood of Jesus, the Son of God. When Jesus died on the cross, God died there. One line from a famous hymn by Charles Wesley says, "Amazing love! how can it be / That Thou, my God, shouldst die for me?" (*Hymns,* #296). Charles Wesley was strong to point out that his God died for him. Jesus, the God-man, died on the cross for all of us.

Hebrews 9:14 says that Christ offered Himself through the eternal Spirit. Jesus, in Himself alone, could not accomplish His crucifixion. To die on the cross as an offering to God, the Son needed the Spirit. Jesus did not die on the cross alone and separate from the Spirit. The Spirit was one with the Son. The Son died on the cross with the Father and by the Spirit. The Father, the Son, and the Spirit were all involved in the Son's crucifixion. The death of Christ was not only the death of the man Jesus but also the death of the Son with the Father and by the Spirit. Because Christ offered Himself through the eternal Spirit, His death is eternally effective. Our co-crucifixion with Christ on the cross (Gal. 2:20) is realized in the eternal Spirit who indwells us.

IN HIS RESURRECTION

Acts 2:32 says, "This Jesus [the Son] God [including the Father and the Spirit] has raised up." The dead Jesus was raised up by God. Acts 10:40 and 41 show us that, on the one hand, God [including the Father and the Spirit] raised this One [the Son] on the third day; on the other hand, He [the Son] rose from the dead. Regarding the Lord as a man, the New Testament tells us that God raised Him from the dead; considering Him as God, it tells us that He Himself rose from the dead. Romans 8:11 refers to "the Spirit of the One [the Triune God] who raised Jesus [the Son] from the dead." The One who raised Jesus did the raising by the Spirit. These verses show us that the Divine Trinity was involved in the resurrection.

IN HIS ASCENSION

The Divine Trinity can also be seen in the Son's ascension. According to Acts 1:11 and 1 Peter 3:22, Jesus Christ [the Son] went into heaven. In His ascension "[the Triune] God highly exalted Him [the Son]" (Phil. 2:9).

IN HIS SALVATION

Our Savior God [the Triune God] saved us, through the renewing of the Holy Spirit, whom He poured out upon us richly through Jesus Christ [the Son] our Savior (Titus 3:4-6). According to Colossians 1:12-13, the Father delivered us. First Timothy 1:15 says that Christ Jesus [the Son] came into the world to save sinners. John 3:5 says that unless one is born of the Spirit, he cannot enter into the kingdom of God. Thus, the Father, the Son, and the Spirit all participated in our salvation.

IN THE CHRISTIAN LIFE

In the Christian life the believers possess the Divine Trinity and should live in and with the Divine Trinity. The Father is in the believers (Eph. 4:6), the Son lives in the believers (Gal. 2:20), and the Spirit abides in the believers (John 14:17). In 2 Corinthians 13:14 Paul says, "The grace of the Lord Jesus Christ [the Son] and the love of God [the Father] and the fellowship of the Holy Spirit be with you all." Then Jude tells us that we should be those who, praying in the Holy Spirit, keep ourselves in the love of God [the Father], awaiting the mercy of our Lord Jesus Christ [the Son] (vv. 20-21).

The revelation of the Divine Trinity in 2 Corinthians 13:14 and Jude 20-21 match each other. In both portions there is the love of God [the Father]. The mercy of our Lord Jesus Christ [the Son] in Jude matches the grace of our Lord Jesus Christ [the Son] in 2 Corinthians. In the Lord Jesus is grace, and when grace is extended to us and reaches us, it is mercy. Finally, praying in the Holy Spirit in Jude matches the fellowship of the Holy Spirit in 2 Corinthians. Praying is a kind of fellowship.

IN THE CHURCH LIFE

We need to see the portions of the Word that reveal the Divine Trinity in the church life. First Corinthians 12:28 reveals that [the Triune] God has placed some in the church: "first apostles, second prophets, third teachers...administrations." Ephesians 4:16 says that out from Christ the Head [the Son] all the Body, being joined together and being knit together through every joint of the rich supply and through the operation in the measure of each one part, causes the growth of the Body unto the building up of itself in love. Acts 20:28 says that the Holy Spirit placed overseers in the church, and 9:31 says that the church went on in the comfort of the Holy Spirit. Finally, Ephesians 4:4 says, "One Body and one Spirit." The Spirit is the reality of the Body of Christ. Hence, if there were no Spirit, there would be no Body of Christ, no church. The reality of the Body of Christ is the Spirit whom we have received, experienced, and enjoyed in many aspects, and the reality of the church life is the very Spirit in whom we live and according to whom we walk.

IN ETERNITY WITHOUT ENDING

The vision of the Divine Trinity in eternity without ending can be seen in the last two chapters of the book of Revelation. Revelation 21 shows that the New Jerusalem as the tabernacle of [the Triune] God will be with men (v. 3); the tabernacle of God will be the wife of the Lamb [the Son] (v. 9); and [the Triune] God will be the light, and the Lamb [the Son] will be the lamp of the city (v. 23). Revelation 22 says that the Spirit will be with the bride (v. 17) and that out of the throne of [the Triune] God and of the Lamb [the Son] will proceed the river of water of life [the Spirit] with the tree of life [the Son] producing twelve fruits (vv. 1-2).

The Triune God—the Father, the Son, and the Spirit—was in eternity without beginning, in creation, in incarnation, in the living and work in Jesus' humanity, in His crucifixion, in His resurrection, and in His ascension. He is also in His salvation, in the Christian life, in the church life, and in eternity without ending. In order for us to live in and with the Divine Trinity, we need to have a vision concerning the Divine Trinity. If we have the Son, we have the Spirit and the Father. If we worship the Father, we also worship the Son and the Spirit because the three are one. We need to live in and with the Divine Trinity, having Him as the very substance and element of our living.

CHAPTER TWO

THE VISION CONCERNING THE ECONOMY OF THE DIVINE TRINITY

Scripture Reading: Eph. 1:9-11; 3:2-11

MYSTERY, WILL, GOOD PLEASURE, PURPOSE, DISPENSATION, AND COUNSEL

Ephesians 1:9-11 says, "Making known to us the mystery of His will according to His good pleasure, which He purposed in Himself, unto the economy of the fullness of the times, to head up all things in Christ, the things in the heavens and the things on the earth, in Him; in whom also we were designated as an inheritance, having been predestinated according to the purpose of the One who works all things according to the counsel of His will." There are six crucial items in these verses: mystery, will, good pleasure, purpose, economy, and counsel. We need to know how to arrange these six items in a proper sequence. The good pleasure of God comes first. God's good pleasure is a matter in His heart. Out of this good pleasure, God made up His mind to do something, and this is His will. According to His will, He had a council in eternity past to make a counsel. There was a council held by God in His divine person, the Trinity, in eternity past in order to make a decision, which is His determined will. This determined will is the counsel. Two items are "of His will"—the mystery of His will and the counsel of His will. The counsel of His will was not revealed but hidden in God, so it became a mystery. The mystery is the counsel, and the counsel is the mystery.

Then according to this counsel, the Triune God made a purpose. This purpose becomes God's *oikonomia,* God's economy, God's dispensation. According to our usage, *dispensation* is different from *dispensing. Dispensation* refers to God's plan, and *dispensing* refers to the actual dispensing of God into His chosen and redeemed people. Dr. C. I. Scofield, in his reference Bible, says that there are seven dispensations: the dispensations of innocence, conscience, human government, promise, law, grace, and the kingdom. That means that God has seven plans, and these seven plans are seven different dealings of God with man in different periods of time. This understanding of the word *dispensation* is correct, but we have also seen something further and deeper concerning the real meaning of this word. God's dispensation, God's economy, is His divine plan to dispense Himself with all His divine riches into His chosen and redeemed people. This economy, *oikonomia,* which was hidden in God, is a mystery.

We may use an illustration of a person planning a trip to show the meaning of good pleasure, will, counsel, purpose, economy, and mystery. A brother may have a desire to attend a training in Irving. To come to Irving to attend a training is a good pleasure in him. Out of this pleasure he makes up his mind. This is his will. Then he has a council with his wife and children. The whole family agrees with his desire to come to Irving. Thus, out of this council a decision is made, which is the counsel. According to this counsel, he makes a plan, and this plan is his purpose. This purpose becomes his *oikonomia,* which is hidden from the brothers in Irving, so it is a mystery to them. But when this brother arrives in Irving, this mystery is revealed to the brothers in Irving by his presence.

In eternity past God had a good pleasure, and His good pleasure is to dispense Himself into His chosen people in order to produce an organism, which is the church as the Body of Christ, for His full, perfect, complete, and eternal expression. We all need to have a vision of God's good pleasure. Even human beings have a good pleasure. If you do not have a good pleasure, there is no reason for you to live. A person enjoys his life because there is a good pleasure in his life. The term *good pleasure* is used twice in Ephesians 1. Verse 5 says, "Predestinating us unto sonship through Jesus Christ to Himself, according to the good pleasure of His will." God's good pleasure is related to His predestination of us. Verse 9 says, "Making known to us the mystery of His will according to His good pleasure, which

He purposed in Himself." God's good pleasure is related to His heart concerning us. When He thought about us as the object of His dispensing, He was happy.

God's good pleasure became the divine will. This will was discussed in the council of the Divine Trinity to become the counsel of His will (v. 11), and this determined will became a plan, a purpose, which is the New Testament *oikonomia,* God's economy. God kept this economy hidden within Himself for many years, so it was a mystery. It was a mystery until the apostles were raised up, especially the apostle Paul. This mystery was revealed to them in their spirit, the human spirit regenerated, indwelt by, and mingled with the Holy Spirit (3:5). It is in our spirit that we can see the divine revelation of God's good pleasure, which eventually became God's economy, God's eternal plan.

THE VISION OF GOD'S ECONOMY

We need to see the vision concerning the economy of the Divine Trinity. We have seen that this economy is a plan, an arrangement (v. 9b; 1:10). Paul uses the word *oikonomia* in Ephesians, 1 Timothy, Colossians, and 1 Corinthians. In 1 Timothy 1:3-4 Paul urges Timothy to remain in Ephesus to charge certain ones not to teach different things from God's economy, which is in faith. This economy is not in the law but in faith. The law represents the Old Testament. All the things written by Moses in the first five books of the Bible, the Pentateuch, are in the law. But whatever Paul ministered as God's economy is in faith. Paul told Timothy to charge certain ones not to teach different things. The main different thing taught by these ones was the law. Paul, however, said that the economy of God ministered by him was not in the law but in faith.

God's economy is in faith. It is not by our doing but by our faith in God's grace. It is not by our doing in ourselves but by our believing in Christ, the embodiment of the Triune God. In the Lord's ministry, we are not teaching the saints to observe something, to keep something, or to do something. We are ministering to the saints something that needs the exercise of their faith. Faith does not originate from us. Faith originates from what we see. When we see God's economy, this generates and initiates a believing within us. God's economy is God's will to dispense Himself into you and me to produce an organism, the Body of Christ, for His good pleasure. Faith comes from seeing this vision. We need a vision, a seeing. We need to see that in the whole universe God's good pleasure is to impart Himself, to dispense Himself, into us so that we may become parts of His organism, the organic Body of Christ. A dispensary is a place where medicine is dispensed to sick patients. God Himself is a dispensary, and He is also an all-inclusive dose, dispensing Himself into us, His patients.

The apostle Paul's teaching begins from God's heart, not from man's fall. His teaching shows us the good pleasure that God has had since eternity past. God's desire is not merely to save sinners but to impart, to dispense, Himself into us as all our need. His dispensing is not only to heal us but also to make us His organism, His living Body. In eternity past God had the desire to dispense Himself into His chosen people to make them all the Body of His embodiment, Christ. This Body is the very organism of the Head, Christ. Our physical body is an organism to match us and to complete us in order to express us in a full and adequate way. In the same way, the Body of Christ is His completion for His full expression.

We need to go to visit people with the gospel in order to carry out God's economy. God needs people as vessels (Rom. 9:21, 23), as "bottles," to contain Him as the all-inclusive dose. We go out to visit people with the gospel to gain more bottles for God, and we fill these bottles with God Himself. When I looked at the situation of all the churches in the Lord's recovery in 1984, I saw that there were very few new bottles. We need to be those who are one with God's heart to gain some new bottles, some new people, into whom He can dispense Himself.

God loves us because we are the vessels, the bottles, who have been made by Him in order to contain Him. God does not merely desire to save us because we are fallen. He wants us as vessels for His dispensing. He needs a Body and a wife to match Him. In the universe there is a divine romance. The concluding picture of the entire Bible is a couple, a husband and a wife (Rev. 21:2; 22:17a). The New Jerusalem is actually a divine couple composed of the processed Triune God married to the transformed tripartite man. This divine couple is the issue of the divine dispensing in God's economy. Since I have seen this, my concept concerning God, Christ, the church, and the believers in Christ has been revolutionized. We need such a vision of God's economy, which is altogether in faith.

GOD'S ECONOMY, PLAN, ARRANGEMENT

The economy of the Divine Trinity, which is His plan, or arrangement, was made by God [the Father and the Spirit] according to God's purpose of the ages [eternal] in Christ Jesus our Lord [the Son] (Eph. 3:11). God's economy is to have us designated as an inheritance, predestinated according to the counsel of God's will (1:11). We are God's vessels, God's bottles, so we are His inheritance, His possession. He possessed us as His inheritance for the purpose of containing Him. He desires to dispense Himself into us all the time. This dispensing is not once for all. It is continuing all the time and will go on for eternity. God has made us His inheritance for His enjoyment. We are God's inheritance by being His vessels. His containers are His inheritance. He needs more vessels into which He can dispense Himself with all His riches.

God made known to us the mystery of His will according to His good pleasure, which He purposed in Himself (v. 9b). God's economy was a mystery hidden from the ages in Himself, who created all things (3:9c, 5a), but it is revealed now to His holy apostles and prophets in spirit [mingled with the Spirit] and is brought to light to all men (vv. 5b, 9a). Such a mingled spirit is the means by which the New Testament revelation concerning God's economy is revealed to the apostles and prophets. We need to be in this spirit to see such a revelation.

The apostle Paul had a clear vision of God's economy, but I am concerned that His economy is still a hidden mystery to many Christians. Paul says in Ephesians that he had been commissioned to reveal, to make known, to bring to light, the mystery of God's economy. To reveal is to make known, and to make known is to enlighten, to bring to light. There are many Christians who have never been enlightened concerning God's economy. Such a mystery has not been made known to them. We need to pray that God's economy would not remain a mystery to us and that we would be enlightened with the truth and the vision of His economy.

THE MYSTERY OF CHRIST

We need a revelation of the mystery of Christ (v. 4), which is the church produced out of the unsearchable riches of Christ. Paul preached the unsearchable riches of Christ as the gospel to the nations [Gentiles], making the nations fellow heirs, fellow members of the Body, and fellow partakers of the promise (v. 6b). Through the church God's multifarious wisdom is made known, especially to the rulers and the authorities of Satan's dark kingdom in the heavenlies (v. 10). The economy that God purposed in Himself is to head up all things in Christ at the fullness of the times (1:10). When the New Jerusalem comes in the new heaven and the new earth, all things will be headed up in Christ through the church.

THE APOSTLES' STEWARDSHIP OF GOD'S GRACE

The economy of the Divine Trinity became the apostles' stewardship of God's grace. Ephesians 3:2 says, "If indeed you have heard of the stewardship of the grace of God which was given to me for you." The word for *stewardship* here and for *economy* in 1:10 is *oikonomia*. *Oikonomia* was first God's plan, God's economy. Then this economy of God became the stewardship that God gave to the apostle Paul. The economy and the stewardship are actually one. This means that what the apostles were doing is what God is doing in His economy. What we are doing should be exactly what God is doing today. We should be those who are carrying out God's economy. The carrying out of God's economy is the stewardship of God's grace. Such a stewardship is for the dispensing of God Himself as grace to all His chosen people. Out of this stewardship comes the ministry of the apostles, and this ministry corresponds with God's economy. The ministry we have must correspond with God's dispensing of Himself into His chosen people for the producing of the Body of Christ. This is God's ministry given to us as our stewardship. The ministry revealed in the New Testament is unique. God does not have two economies or two stewardships. God has only one divine economy and one divine stewardship. Out of this stewardship is the one, unique ministry of the apostles to dispense Christ as God's grace into His chosen people for the building up of the church as the Body of Christ to be the organism of the processed Triune God for His full and eternal expression.

FAITH VERSUS THE LAW

We have pointed out that God's economy is not in the law but in faith. Galatians 3 is a chapter concerning the contrast between the Spirit by faith versus the flesh by law. Many believers in the province of Galatia had been distracted by the Judaizers from the New Testament faith to the Old Testament law. The Judaizers were those who were telling people that in addition to believing in Jesus, they still needed to keep the law. This forced the apostle Paul to write his letter to the Galatians. Galatians 3:1-2 says, "O foolish Galatians, who has bewitched you, before whose eyes Jesus Christ was openly portrayed crucified? This only I wish to learn from you, Did you receive the Spirit out of the works of law or out of the hearing of faith?" The Spirit is the unique blessing of the New Testament gospel, the consummated Triune God dispensed into our being. The Galatians received the Spirit out of the hearing of faith, not out of the works of the law. Footnote 3 on Galatians 3:2 in the Recovery Version says,

> The law was the basic condition for the relationship between man and God in God's Old Testament economy (v. 23); faith is the unique way for God to carry out His New Testament economy with man (1 Tim. 1:4). The law is related to the flesh (Rom. 7:5) and depends on the effort of the flesh, the very flesh that is the expression of the "I." Faith is related to the Spirit and trusts in the operation of the Spirit, the very Spirit who is the realization of Christ. In the Old Testament the "I" and the flesh played an important role in the keeping of the law. In the New Testament Christ and the Spirit take over the position of the "I" and the flesh, and faith replaces the law, that we may live Christ by the Spirit. To keep the law by the flesh is man's natural way; it is in the darkness of man's concept and results in death and wretchedness (Rom.

7:10-11, 24). To receive the Spirit out of the hearing of faith is God's revealed way; it is in the light of God's revelation and issues in life and glory (Rom. 8:2, 6, 10-11, 30). Hence, we must treasure the hearing of faith, not the works of law. It is by the hearing of faith that we received the Spirit so that we might participate in God's promised blessing and live Christ.

In 1 Timothy 1:3-4 Paul told Timothy to charge certain ones not to teach things other than God's economy. This economy is in faith, not in the law. It does not belong to the law in the Old Testament. But it altogether belongs to the New Testament faith, which is the contents of the entire New Testament. The divine economy in faith must be made fully clear to the saints in the administration and shepherding of a local church.

Our seeing of the divine economy is a matter of degree. Thirty years ago I saw something concerning His economy, His heart's desire, but I did not see it then as deeply as I see it today. I believe that after another period of time the Lord will show me more. Related to the depth of our seeing, the hardship is in our understanding. This is why Paul prayed that we believers would have a spirit of wisdom and revelation (Eph. 1:17). We need the seeing spirit and the understanding wisdom. Whatever we do must be based upon the vision of God's economy.

The

CHAPTER THREE

THE VISION CONCERNING
THE DISPENSING OF THE DIVINE TRINITY

Scripture Reading: John 1:14, 16; 3:16; 1 John 4:9; Gal. 4:4; Rom. 8:3; John 6:32, 40; 5:24; Heb. 2:14; 1 Tim. 3:16; John 1:17b; 10:10b; 19:34; Titus 2:14; Matt. 26:26; John 6:32-33, 48-51, 57b; Rev. 2:17; 1 Cor. 10:3; Rev. 2:7; 22:2; Eph. 3:8; 1 Cor. 15:45b; 2 Cor. 3:6; Rom. 8:11; Phil. 1:19-21a; Rev. 22:1; 1 Cor. 12:13; 10:4

In the first two chapters we saw the vision concerning the Divine Trinity and the vision concerning the economy of the Divine Trinity. In this chapter we want to see the vision concerning the dispensing of the Divine Trinity. The dispensing of the Divine Trinity is included in His economy. God's economy is His household administration. In ancient times a large family of perhaps a few generations would live together. Such a large family was in need of an administration, an arrangement, for the food to be dispensed to them. In the Old Testament Joseph is a good example of a household administrator, a steward. He was the administrator of Pharaoh's house. The supply of food was under Joseph's stewardship. His stewardship was to dispense the food to all those in Pharaoh's house.

We must see the distinction between the terms *dispensation* and *dispensing*. God's dispensation, His economy, is His plan to dispense Himself as the rich supply to all of His chosen people. In God's dispensation, God intends to dispense Himself into His people. Dispensing is imparting, distributing, and giving. God is giving Himself, imparting Himself, distributing Himself, dispensing Himself, into His people for their enjoyment. This dispensing is of the Triune God—of the Father, of the Son, and of the Spirit.

THE DISPENSING OF THE TRIUNE GOD

The Triune God Becoming Flesh and Tabernacling among Us, Full of Grace and Reality

The dispensing of the Triune God can first be seen in John 1:14 and 16. These verses tell us that the Word [the Triune God] became flesh and tabernacled among us, full of grace and reality, and that of His fullness we have all received, and grace upon grace. What was the purpose of the Triune God becoming flesh and tabernacling among us? It is correct to say that the Triune God became incarnated to be our Savior, but this is too superficial. We need to realize that John 1:14 is like a big ocean. Its significance is deep, broad, and beyond our natural understanding. This verse is also like a deep mine full of treasures.

John 1:14 says that the incarnated Triune God was full of grace and reality. Many Christians do not have a proper realization of what grace and reality are. Grace is God Himself for our enjoyment. Two lines from *Hymns,* #497 say, "Grace in its highest definition is / God in the Son to be enjoyed by us." Grace is God being enjoyed by us, and reality is God being realized by us. Grace is God for our enjoyment, and reality is God for our possession. Nothing is real in the universe except God. The real light is our God. Our real drink is God. Our food is God. God is the reality. The phrase *full of grace and reality* in verse 14 indicates that the incarnation is for God to come to dispense Himself into us as our enjoyment and as our possession. We need to see such a great vision. The incarnation of the Divine Trinity is for the dispensing of Himself into us for our enjoyment and for our inheritance. In His dispensing we enjoy Him and inherit Him as our possession, as our reality.

Revelation 21 and 22 reveal that in the New Jerusalem in eternity future, God will be our unique reality. The city has no need of the sun or of the moon because God Himself is the light, and Christ is the lamp (21:23; 22:5). The light in the universe will not be something made by man but will be God Himself. God is the reality of light, and He is our possession, our inheritance. In the New Jerusalem there is also the river of water of life (v. 1). This river is a symbol of the Spirit as the supply of the divine and spiritual water to meet our need. Our food in the New Jerusalem will be the fruit of the tree of life (v. 2). Thus, in the New Jerusalem the light is God Himself, the water is God Himself, and the food is God Himself. He is the reality of these necessities. God came in incarnation with all these riches of grace and reality. We enjoy and inherit Him as such a rich supply.

The Triune God So Loving the World That He Gave His Only Begotten Son, That Everyone Who Believes into Him Would Have Eternal Life

John 3:16 says that [the Triune] God so loved the world that He gave His only begotten Son, that everyone who believes into Him would have eternal life. *The world* in this verse refers to mankind. God so loved mankind that He gave His only begotten Son for what purpose? It was so that everyone who believes into the Son would have eternal life. God gave His Son, and we receive eternal life. He loved mankind to such an extent that He gave His only begotten Son to us. Then we receive eternal life by believing into His dear Son. God's giving His Son to us is His dispensing. The Son is the embodiment of the Father. When the Father gave His Son to us, that was God giving Himself in His embodiment to us. If we receive His Son, His embodiment, we receive eternal life. This indicates that eternal life is the Son, the embodiment of the Triune God. To receive eternal life is to receive the Son as the embodiment of the Triune God, as a gift from Him.

The Triune God Sending His Son into the World, Born of a Woman, That We Might Have Life and Live through Him

First John 4:9 says that [the Triune] God sent His only begotten Son into the world that we might have life and live through Him. This verse reveals the dispensing of the Triune God in the Son that we might have Him as life and live through Him. Galatians 4:4 says that [the Triune] God sent forth His Son, born of a woman. God dispensed Himself into us as the gift of life through incarnation by being born into a woman.

The Triune God Sending His Own Son
in the Likeness of the Flesh of Sin

Romans 8:3 says that [the Triune] God sent His own Son in the likeness of the flesh of sin. By sending His Son in the likeness of the flesh of sin, God came to dispense Himself into us as the gift of eternal life. The truth in Romans 8:3 can be seen in the type of the bronze serpent in Numbers 21, referred to by the Lord Jesus in John 3:14: "As Moses lifted up the serpent in the wilderness, so must the Son of Man be lifted up." The bronze serpent lifted up by Moses was in the likeness of a serpent, but within it there was not the poison of a serpent. Likewise, Christ was in the likeness of the flesh of sin, but within Him there was no sin. By being lifted up on the cross as the bronze serpent, Christ dealt with Satan, the old serpent (12:31-33; Heb. 2:14). This means that the serpentine nature within fallen man has been dealt with so that man might have eternal life. This is the way that the Triune God came to dispense Himself into His chosen people.

THE DISPENSING OF THE FATHER

The dispensing of the Father can be seen in the Gospel of John. Verse 32 of chapter 6 says that the Father gives us the true bread out of heaven. The Lord Jesus told us clearly that He is the very bread from heaven given by the Father. This means that the Father is dispensing Christ as food to all of us. John 6:40 says that the will of the Father is that everyone who beholds the Son and believes into Him should have eternal life. Christ as the heavenly bread dispensed to us is the embodiment of the eternal life. When we receive this bread and eat it, we have this bread within us as the eternal life. The Father gives us the heavenly bread, which signifies the Son. Thus, the Son is the heavenly food for our life supply.

We can also see the dispensing of the Father in John 8:29, which says that He [the Father] who sent the Son is with the Son. The Father gives the Son as the heavenly bread, but when He gives the Son, He comes with the Son. The Father who sent the Son is with the Son. The natural thought is that the Father remained in the heavens when He sent the Son to us to be our food supply. But according to the divine revelation, the Father was with the Son when the Son came. This shows that not only the Son but also the Father is the component of the heavenly bread. When we receive the Son, we have the Father with the Son as our food supply. This is the dispensing of the Father.

John 5:24 says that he who hears the Son and believes the Father who sent the Son has eternal life. The book of John repeatedly tells us that God has given Himself for us to receive Him as our eternal life. This giving and receiving indicates the dispensing of the Father.

THE DISPENSING OF THE SON

Now we want to see the dispensing of the Son. The Son, who shared in our blood and flesh, was manifested in the flesh (Heb. 2:14; 1 Tim. 3:16). As we have seen, the Son was born of a woman in the likeness of the flesh of sin. The dispensing of the Son is also seen in grace and reality coming through Jesus Christ (John 1:17b). Jesus Christ came for the purpose of dispensing God Himself as grace and reality to us. God Himself as grace and reality came through Jesus Christ. This is the dispensing of the Son.

The Son came that we may have life and have life abundantly (10:10b). He desired to dispense Himself into us as life. This can also be seen in John 19:34, which says that one of the soldiers pierced His side, and immediately there came out blood and water. The blood is for our redemption, and the water is for God's dispensing. The blood deals with sins, and the water is the flow of the divine life to quench our thirst and swallow up our death. The water is for the dispensing of the divine life into our being. The Son of God loved us and gave Himself for us (Gal. 2:20; Titus 2:14). His giving of Himself was for His dispensing.

The Son gave Himself to us that we might eat Him. When the Lord Jesus established His table, He gave the bread to the disciples and said, "Take, eat; this is My body" (Matt. 26:26). This shows us that to remember the Lord at His table is to enjoy Him by eating Him. The Lord Jesus, who gave Himself on the cross for us, is edible. The bread on our dining table has been processed, or cooked. After the cross our Lord is now the heavenly bread who has been cooked. Now this bread is ready for us to take and eat. Today Jesus is edible. The Lord's table, of which we partake, is a sign, a symbol, of our daily walk, indicating that

our daily walk is one of taking Christ as our life supply and living by this supply. One day a week we come together to give
a testimony to the entire universe with a declaration that this
is the way we live. We live by eating Jesus as our food, our life
supply. We need to see the vision of Jesus being edible.

The Son is our life supply as manna, even the hidden manna
(John 6:32-33, 48-51, 57b; 1 Cor. 10:3). In John 6 the Lord compared Himself to the heavenly manna that was given to the
children of Israel in ancient times. In the seven epistles in Revelation written by the Lord Jesus to His seven churches, Jesus
is revealed as the hidden manna (2:17). He is the real manna
for our life supply.

The Son is also our life supply as the tree of life with its fruit
(v. 7; 22:2). The tree of life is seen in both Genesis and Revelation. In Revelation 2:7 the tree of life is promised as a reward to
the overcomers. In Revelation 22:2, 14, and 19 it is a complete
fulfillment of God's intention in Genesis. In eternity future we
will be in the New Jerusalem enjoying Christ as our life supply,
as the fruit of the tree of life.

Eating results in the mingling of divinity with humanity. In
the early church there was a heretical teaching concerning the
mingling, which said that the mingling of divinity and humanity produces a third nature. Because of this heresy nearly everyone avoided the truth concerning mingling. But in the Bible
there is a strong revelation concerning the mingling of the divine
nature with the human nature. This is typified by the meal offering in the Old Testament, composed of fine flour mingled with
oil (Lev. 2:4-5). The fine flour signifies humanity, and the oil signifies the Holy Spirit with His divinity. Oil mingled with fine
flour signifies that divinity is mingled with humanity. There is
a third entity produced but not a third nature. This third entity
is not merely oil or fine flour but a cake made of oil mingled with
fine flour, signifying the mingling of divinity with humanity.
After this mingling these two natures remain distinguishable.
They remain two natures without a third nature being produced.
Thus, there is a third entity but not a third nature.

Whatever we eat, digest, and assimilate is mingled with us
and even becomes us. This is why dietitians say that we are what
we eat. A little boy becomes big and strong by being mingled with

what he eats. What we eat is assimilated into us and eventually becomes our very fiber and tissue. In John 6:57 the Lord said that he who eats Him shall live because of Him. God in Christ is good for food. His being food is for the dispensing of Himself into our being.

The dispensing of the Son is also seen in Ephesians 3:8, which reveals that the unsearchable riches of Christ [the Son] are for the New Testament ministry in the divine dispensing. Many people claim that they have a ministry, which is a service, but what is the content of their service? Do we minister Christ as the food supply to His believers? If we do not, we do not have a real, genuine, adequate ministry. The real, genuine, adequate ministry in the New Testament is the divine stewardship that ministers the Triune God in Christ to people as their life and life supply. In all the messages I have given throughout the years, my unique burden has been to minister Christ to God's people as their life and life supply. This truth is expressed in *Hymns,* #509, the chorus of which says,

> God is in Christ to be my supply,
> God as the Spirit nourisheth me;
> If upon Christ in spirit I feed,
>   Filled with His life I'll be.

THE DISPENSING OF THE SPIRIT

First Corinthians 15:45b shows us the life-giving Spirit for the divine dispensing. The consummated Triune God is the life-giving Spirit. Life-giving means life-imparting, and life-imparting means dispensing. The consummated Spirit of the Triune God is dispensing the divine life into us all day long. The Spirit gives life (2 Cor. 3:6).

The Spirit of the One who raised Jesus from the dead gives life to our mortal bodies (Rom. 8:11). The life-giving Spirit first gives life to our spirit (v. 10). Then from our spirit He spreads the divine life into our soul to transform us (v. 6). Eventually, He gives life to our mortal body. We do not need to wait for this. Even today when we are sick, we can exercise our faith to say, "Lord, send Your Spirit from my spirit into my body to enliven it. My body is now weak and sick. It may even be dying. But Lord, I ask

You to dispense Your life through the life-giving Spirit into my mortal and dying body. I need Your divine life." We need to exercise our faith to live not by ourselves but by Him. We live by Jesus. We have a dying life, but He is not dying. The Spirit of the One who raised Jesus from the dead gives life to our dying body. This is dispensing.

The bountiful supply of the Spirit is for us to live and magnify Christ (Phil. 1:19-21). God has prepared such a bountiful supply for dispensing. Furthermore, the Spirit is the flow of the life supply as the river of water of life that we might drink Him (Rev. 22:1; 1 Cor. 12:13; 10:4). Eating and drinking are for dispensing. In 1965 we had a conference with a training on eating and drinking Jesus. This truth is seen throughout the entire Bible. In Genesis 2 is the eating of the tree of life. In Exodus is the eating of the lamb in Egypt and the eating of manna and drinking of the water that flowed out of the cleft rock in the wilderness. When the people of Israel entered into the good land, they ate the produce of that land. The offerings in Leviticus are for God's eating and our eating. This is all the eating of Jesus in typology. Then in the New Testament Jesus Himself told us that He is the heavenly bread and that we need to eat Him (John 6:51, 57).

In Matthew 15 there is a story of the Lord's encounter with a Canaanite woman. When she asked the Lord to help her, He replied, "It is not good to take the children's bread and throw it to the little dogs" (v. 26). Then she said, "Yes, Lord, for even the little dogs eat of the crumbs which fall from their masters' table" (v. 27). The Canaanite woman, not offended by the Lord's word but rather, admitting that she was a heathen dog, considered that at that time Christ, after being rejected by the children, the Jews, became crumbs under the table as a portion to the Gentiles. The holy land of Israel was the table on which Christ, the heavenly bread, came as a portion to the children of Israel. But they threw Him off the table to the ground, the Gentile country, so that He became broken crumbs as a portion to the Gentiles. This shows us again that God is for our eating so that He can dispense Himself into us and mingle Himself with us that He and we may become one.

CHAPTER FOUR

PORTIONS IN THE NEW TESTAMENT REVEALING THE DIVINE TRINITY IN THE DIVINE MOVE AND IN OUR EXPERIENCE

(1)

Scripture Reading: Eph. 1:3-14; 1 Pet. 1:2; Luke 1:35; Matt. 1:20-23; John 14:6-24, 26; 15:26; 16:13-15

In this chapter we want to fellowship more concerning the revelation of the Divine Trinity. We want to see the portions in the New Testament revealing the Divine Trinity in the divine move and in our experience.

EPHESIANS 1:3

Ephesians 1:3 says, "Blessed be the God and Father of our Lord Jesus Christ [the Son], who has blessed us with every spiritual blessing [blessing of the Spirit] in the heavenlies in Christ [the Son]." Ephesians 1:3 is a leading portion of the Word concerning the revelation of the Divine Trinity. This verse reveals the Divine Trinity—the Father, the Son, and the Spirit. In this verse the Father is the source of the divine blessing to us.

Then the Spirit is the nature and essence of the divine blessing. The divine blessing we have received is of a spiritual nature and a spiritual source. The divine Father is the source of this blessing, and the divine Spirit is the nature and the essence of this divine blessing we have received.

Third, the Son is the sphere, the element, and the means of the divine blessing. Within the sphere of the Son, God gave us His divine blessing. Christ is also the element of the divine blessing. An element is a substance, and every substance has its essence with its nature. Wood, for example, is an element. In this element are a nature and an essence. The nature and essence of the divine blessing are of the Spirit, but the very element of this blessing is Christ Himself. When we say that Christ is the element of God's blessing, we are saying that Christ Himself is the divine blessing. In this divine blessing are the spiritual nature and the spiritual essence. Christ, the Son Himself, is the blessing, the Spirit is the nature and essence of this blessing, and the Father is the source who gives this blessing.

EPHESIANS 1:4-14

Ephesians 1:4-14 reveals the Father, the Son, and the Spirit, moving to dispense Himself into us. First, verses 4 through 6 show us the Father's selection and predestination for God's eternal purpose. The Father's selection is His choosing, and His predestination is His marking out. His selection and predestination are for the fulfillment of His eternal purpose, His eternal plan. We feel that a better translation of verses 4 and 5 is as follows: "Even as He chose us in Him before the foundation of the world to be holy and without blemish before Him in love, predestinating us unto sonship through Jesus Christ to Himself, according to the good pleasure of His will." God's choosing includes His predestinating. How did God choose us? He chose us by predestinating us. When someone goes to the supermarket, he may select something and then mark it out. His marking it out is the action of his selecting. Actually, his marking out is his selection. God the Father selected us by marking us out before the foundation of the world.

Verses 7 through 12 of Ephesians 1 go on to reveal the Son's redemption for the accomplishment of God's eternal purpose. God the Father chose us. Then the Son came to accomplish God's economy by His redemption. We were chosen and predestinated, but after creation we became fallen. Hence, we need redemption, which God has accomplished for us in Christ through His blood.

Verses 13 and 14 reveal the Spirit's sealing and pledging for the application of God's accomplished purpose. First, God has an eternal purpose. For this purpose God selected us. Then the Son came to accomplish this purpose by His redemption. After the accomplishment of the Son's redemption, the Spirit comes to apply what the Son has accomplished according to the Father's selection. This application is by the Spirit's sealing and pledging.

A proper sealing cannot take place without the element of ink. A seal also bears an image. When a seal with ink is applied to something, the ink will be in the same form or image as the seal. If the seal is round, the impression made is also round. The seal is God Himself, and the ink is the Spirit. The sealing of the Spirit causes us to bear God's image, thus making us like God.

Furthermore, this sealing is also the pledging. God has pledged Himself to us and in us for our security, our guarantee that He belongs to us, and for our foretaste in participating in Him as our inheritance—enjoyment. When a person buys a new Bible, he may put his seal with his signature on it. This seal on his Bible displays the fact that the Bible is his. In another sense the seal becomes a pledge to guarantee that the Bible belongs to him. Thus, we may say that the sealing is the pledging. Now we can see that Ephesians 1:4-14 reveals that the Triune God has been wrought into us for the fulfillment of His eternal economy.

FIRST PETER 1:2

First Peter 1:2 shows us the working of the Divine Trinity. In this verse are the foreknowledge of God the Father, the sanctification of the Spirit, and the sprinkling of the blood of Jesus Christ [the Son]. The Father as the source foreknew us. Following the Father's foreknowledge, the Spirit came to sanctify us. His sanctifying work was to separate us and bring us back to God. This is the aspect of the Holy Spirit's sanctification before Christ's redemption. Then there is the sprinkling of the blood of Jesus Christ, the Son, indicating Christ's redemption. The sanctification of the Spirit is divided into three stages. The first is for our repentance, the second is for our justification, and the third is for our transformation. In the book of Romans Christ's redemption is revealed first and then the Holy Spirit's sanctification. But in 1 Peter 1:2 the sanctification of the Spirit is first, and then the sprinkling of the blood of Jesus Christ follows this sanctification. This is why we need to see the different aspects and stages of the sanctification of the Spirit.

In Luke 15 the Lord Jesus told three parables. In the first parable the good shepherd goes to find the lost sheep. The second parable is that of a woman seeking her lost coin. The third parable reveals a loving father receiving a returning prodigal son. These three parables reveal the Divine Trinity. The Son is the good shepherd, the Holy Spirit is the seeking woman, and God the Father is the loving and receiving father. In Luke 15 the seeking woman lights a lamp, sweeps the house, and seeks carefully until she finds her lost coin (vv. 8, 10, 17). This typifies the sanctifying work of the Holy Spirit. He enlightens us from within and searches out our sins one by one that we may know our sins and repent.

This sanctification of the Holy Spirit causes us to turn to the Lord and receive God's full salvation. Before we received the Lord, we were living in the world with the worldly people. But one day the Spirit came to find us, to separate us unto God, even before we were redeemed. He sanctified us, separated us unto God, before we were forgiven of our sins and justified by God the Father. His sanctifying work separated us unto God so that we would come to ourselves (v. 17), repent, and turn to God (Acts 26:20).

The seeking of the woman in Luke 15 typifies the initial sanctification of the Spirit, which is the sanctification of the Spirit revealed in 1 Peter 1:2. Thus, we can see that 1 Peter 1:2 unveils the divine economy through the operation of the trinity of the Godhead for the believers' participation in the Triune God. God the Father's selection is the initiation; God the Spirit's sanctification carries out the selection of God the Father; and God the Son's redemption, signified by the sprinkling of His blood, is the completion.

LUKE 1:35

Luke 1:35 is a verse concerning the divine conception of the Lord Jesus. In this divine conception the Divine Trinity is revealed. Luke 1:35 shows the Holy Spirit's coming upon Mary; the Most High [God the Father] overshadowing Mary; and the birth of the holy thing [the Son of God]. Thus, the entire Divine Trinity was involved in the conception of the Man-Savior.

MATTHEW 1:20-23

Matthew 1:20-23 also refers to the birth of Jesus, the Son of God. Verses 20 and 21 show us the divine conception of the Holy Spirit and the birth of Jesus [the Son]. Then verse 23 tells us that this One was called by men Emmanuel, which means "God [God the Father] with us." These verses again reveal the working of the Divine Trinity in the Savior's incarnation. God the Father's being with us was the issue of the divine conception of the Holy Spirit and the birth of Jesus, the Son.

JOHN 14:6-24

The Divine Trinity in the divine move and in our experience is revealed also in John 14:6-24. In verse 6 the Lord said, "I am the way and the reality and the life; no one comes to the Father except through Me." This verse shows that the believers come to the Father through the Son—the Father being the object of the believers. John 14—16 records the last conversation that the Lord had with His disciples while He was on this earth. In His last talk to them He indicated that all His believers should seek after the Father. In other words, they should take the Father as their object. If we are going to reach the Father as our object, we must reach Him through the Son, who is the way.

Verses 7 through 14 show the Father embodied in the Son seen among the believers—the Son being the Father's embodiment among the believers. In these verses the Lord showed us that He is in the Father and that the Father is in Him. The Son and the Father are one. They mutually indwell each other. The Son dwells in the Father, and the Father dwells in the Son. In this way the Son was the Father's embodiment among the believers.

Verses 15 through 20 go on to show us the Son realized as the Spirit abiding in the believers—the Spirit being the realization of the Son abiding in the believers. The Father is embodied in the Son, and the Son is realized as the Spirit. The Son as the Father's embodiment was only among the believers, but the Spirit as the realization of the Son is now abiding within the believers. The Father is the object, the Son is the Father's embodiment, and the Spirit is the realization of the Son. The Son as the Father's embodiment was still outside of us. He needed to become the Spirit so that He could abide in the believers. Now that we have the Spirit as the realization of the Son abiding in us, we also have the Father's embodiment and the Father as our object. Actually, the Father as our object is within us, because the object is embodied in the Son and the Son is realized as the Spirit who indwells us. If we have the Spirit, we have the Son, and if we have the Son, we have the Father. Thus, the three of the Divine Trinity are in us.

The Father as the object, the Son as the embodiment, and the Spirit as the realization are in us, the container. As the container, we contain the realization. Within the realization is the embodiment, and within the embodiment is the object. The object, the embodiment, and the realization are the excellent treasure in us, the earthen vessels (2 Cor. 4:7). As earthen vessels, we contain the excellent deity in three aspects.

Verses 21 and 23 of John 14 show the Son manifesting Himself to His lover and the Father coming with Him to make an abode with the Son's lover. After the abiding of the Spirit in us, the Son will manifest Himself to His lovers. It is possible to be a believer of Jesus Christ but not be a lover of Him. When we believe in Him, the three of the Divine Trinity come to abide in us. But after we believe in Him and know that He is abiding in us, we need to love Him. In verses 21 and 23 we see the request of our love toward Him. We may be the believers of Christ, but how many among us are the lovers of Jesus? The Father as the object is in Jesus as the embodiment, this embodiment is in the Spirit as His realization, and this realization is the very Spirit who is now abiding in all of us. But we need to ask whether or not we enjoy the manifestation of the Lord Jesus to us daily and even hourly.

In the morning we may have had a time with the Lord to enjoy His manifestation, but later we might become unhappy with our spouse and lose the Lord's manifestation to us. This, however, does not mean that we have lost the abiding of the Spirit within us. Some Christians feel that when they lose the manifestation of Jesus, they have lost their salvation, but this is not true, because the Spirit always abides in the believers. Those who believe they can lose their salvation actually believe in "elevator salvation." When the "elevator" is up, they are saved. When it is down, they are unsaved. Our salvation, however, is not an elevator but a "stairway," from which we can never be removed. Although we are on this stairway, we want to enjoy the blessing of the top part of the stairway. We want to be on the "top floor," not in the "basement." This is why we need to love the Lord Jesus and say, "Lord Jesus, I love You." As we love Him, we are brought up to the top floor. Then we see everything in the heavens. If we do not love Him, we are at the bottom of the stairway where we can see very little. But this does not mean that we have lost our salvation. We are still on the stairway of His salvation.

When we love Him, not only does His Spirit abide in us but also He Himself will manifest Himself to us. This means that we have the presence of the One whom we love in our fellowship with Him. If we love Jesus, Jesus loves us, and the Father loves us also. When the Son manifests Himself to us, the Father comes with Him to make an abode with us, to stay with us. We need to be brought more and more into the manifestation of the Son to us, with the Father and the Son making an abode with us. We need to go up the stairway of the Lord's salvation by loving Him. Then He will manifest Himself to us, and the Father and the Son will make Their abode with us for our enjoyment.

JOHN 14:26

In John 14:26 we see the Father sending the Comforter, the Holy Spirit, in the Son's name. Now we need to ask what or who is in the Son's name. Does this modifier—*in the Son's name*—modify the Father's sending, or does it modify the sent One? It modifies the Sender, not the sent One. The Father in the Son's name sent the Spirit. The Sender is the Father, but the Father sent in the Son's name. This makes the Sender, the Father, one with the Son. Thus, the Father as the Son sent the Spirit. John 14:26 makes the Father and the Son one in sending the Spirit. The Son is the Father because the Father is in the Son's name.

JOHN 15:26

John 15:26 reveals the Son sending from with the Father the Spirit of reality proceeding from with the Father. The Greek preposition *para,* translated "from" in the Recovery Version, literally means "from with." The Son sent the Spirit from the Father and with the Father. Thus, the Son sent both the Father and the Spirit. When the Spirit was sent, the Father also was sent because the Spirit was sent with the Father.

John 14:26 says that the Father is the Sender, whereas 15:26 says that the Son is the Sender. When we compare these two verses, we see the mystery of the Triune God. According to the proper biblical theology, the three of the Divine Trinity are distinct but not separate. Whereas the Son prays to the Father, He also declares that the Father is in Him and that He is in the Father (14:10). The three of the Godhead coinhere. To coinhere is to indwell mutually. In the Godhead the three coinhere; that is, They dwell within one another. They are three, yet They are still one. This is a mystery.

In the Old Testament, in both Exodus and Zechariah, there is the type of the lampstand. There is one lampstand with seven lamps. The stand is one, and the lamps are seven. Although it is one lampstand, there are seven lamps. Although our Triune God is one God, He is three in His Godhead. The Father, the Son, and the Spirit are distinct, but They are not separate. There is only distinction in the Godhead but no separation. The three of the Godhead are not separate because They dwell in one another. They cannot be separated, but They are distinct because They are the Father, the Son, and the Spirit. Our God is three-one. We need a revelation of our mysterious Triune God in His Divine Trinity.

JOHN 16:13-15

The divine transmission of the Divine Trinity to the believers is revealed in John 16:13-15. This transmission is just like the transmission of electrical current. When the electricity is switched on, there is a current of electricity, a moving of electricity, and that moving is the transmission. First, all that the Father has is the Son's (v. 15). This means that what the Father has is transmitted into the Son. Second, all that the Son has is received by the Spirit (v. 14b). This is a further step of this transmission. The Father transmits to the Son, and then there is a transmitting from the Son to the Spirit. Third, all that the Spirit has received of the Son is disclosed to the believers (vv. 13, 15b). Eventually, all that the Trinity is and has is ours.

Stanza 3 of *Hymns,* #501 talks about this transmission. This stanza says,

> All things of the Father are Thine;
> All Thou art in Spirit is mine;
> The Spirit makes Thee real to me,
> That Thou experienced might be.

This stanza tells us that whatever the Father has is the Son's, whatever the Son is has been received by the Spirit, and then the Spirit discloses to us whatever He has received of the Son. This transmission is from the Father to the Son, from the Son to the Spirit, and from the Spirit to us. This is the move of the Divine Trinity.

CHAPTER FIVE

PORTIONS IN THE NEW TESTAMENT REVEALING THE DIVINE TRINITY IN THE DIVINE MOVE AND IN OUR EXPERIENCE

(2)

Scripture Reading: Matt. 12:28; Heb. 9:14; Matt. 28:19; Heb. 2:3-4; Luke 15:3-32; Eph. 2:18; Titus 3:4-6; 1 John 4:13-14; Gal. 4:4-6; Rom. 8:9; 1 Cor. 12:4-6

In this chapter we want to see more portions in the New Testament revealing the Divine Trinity in the divine move and in our experience. By looking at these portions in the New Testament, we can see that within the Divine Trinity there are many divine excellencies, divine virtues, and divine attributes, such as oneness, humility, beauty, and harmony. In these portions of the Scriptures we need to see the beauties, the excellencies, the virtues, and the attributes of the Godhead in the Divine Trinity.

MATTHEW 12:28

In Matthew 12:28 the Lord said, "If I [the Son], by the Spirit of God [the Triune God including the Father], cast out the demons, then the kingdom of God [the Triune God] has come upon you." Matthew 12:28 seemingly is a simple word, but we need to look into this verse to see its deeper meaning and revelation. We need to ask, "Couldn't the Lord Jesus have cast out these demons by Himself? Couldn't the Lord have said that He cast out demons by Himself in order that His own kingdom might come upon the people? What would have been wrong with this?" If the Son would have done this, He would have acted individualistically. At that time He was among the Pharisees, who were proud, selfish, and individualistic. They would not work with anyone else. There was no humility among them, and they were full of self-seeking, selfishness. Now there was One, condemned by them and standing in front of them, telling them that He did something in a different way. The way He cast out demons showed them that He was humble. He was not individualistic. He was not doing something by Himself and for Himself. He was doing something by the Spirit of God and for the kingdom of God. He never did anything by Himself or for Himself. Is this not beautiful? This shows us the excellency in the Divine Trinity.

This is surely a good pattern for our coordination. The Lord has produced a Body constituted with many members, so all the members should learn of Him. He was working by the Spirit of God for God the Father. He never did anything by Himself or for Himself. Is this not a pattern for us to be coordinated in His Body? We should behave ourselves just like our Head. He behaved Himself in a way of neither doing anything by Himself nor doing anything for Himself. Today in the church life the Body of Christ has not been built up adequately because of the shortage of the proper coordination. If we want to be coordinated with all the members in the Body, we have to learn of Christ our Head, taking Him as our pattern. We should not do anything by ourselves or for ourselves. I may do something according to the will of God, but what I do should not be by myself but by some others. Furthermore, what I do should not be for myself but for the interest, the right, of God on the earth. This is a beauty, and this beauty is a real excellency, a real divine attribute, and an excellent virtue that we need to copy.

I questioned Matthew 12:28 quite often. I wondered why the Lord did not say that He cast out demons by Himself for His own kingdom. Instead, He said that He cast out demons by another One and for another One. His spirit was so humble, so selfless. He did nothing by Himself or for Himself. With Him there was no self, no element of selfishness. This is a beauty.

HEBREWS 9:14

Hebrews 9:14 also reveals the Divine Trinity in His divine move. In this verse there is the blood of Christ [the Son]. There is also Christ, the Son, through the eternal Spirit offering Himself without blemish to God [God the Father]. Finally, this verse says that the blood of Christ purifies our conscience from dead works to serve the living God [the Triune God]. The blood of Christ is the blood of the Son. Also, 1 John 1:7 refers to the blood of Jesus, the Son of God.

Christ offered Himself as one sacrifice to be the reality of all the various offerings to God in the Old Testament. He is the reality of the burnt offering, the meal offering, the peace offering, the sin offering, the trespass offering, the wave offering, the heave offering, the freewill offering, and the drink offering. He is the aggregate reality of all the offerings in the Old Testament as the unique offering to God in the New Testament.

Christ offered Himself to God through the eternal Spirit. In Matthew 12 the Lord cast out demons by the Spirit of God. Hebrews 9:14 says He offered Himself through the eternal Spirit. Again, we need to ask why the Lord did not offer Himself to God by Himself. Was He not qualified to do it? He was qualified, and He could if He would, but He would not. He offered Himself through a channel, through a means, that is, through the eternal Spirit.

Now we need to ask whether the Spirit through whom the Lord offered Himself was the essential Spirit or the economical Spirit. Whether the eternal Spirit here is essential or economical depends upon our definition of what the Lord is doing here. He offered Himself. Was this a work? If this was a work, surely the Spirit through whom Christ offered Himself was economical. Christ did this work through the eternal Spirit for God's economy. The economical Spirit is related to His doing, not His being. On the other hand, His offering of Himself as the unique offering may refer to His being. In relation to His being, the eternal Spirit is the essential Spirit. When the Lord cast out demons, the Spirit by whom He did this was economical. This Spirit was the power, the means, by which the Lord Jesus cast out demons.

In Hebrews 9:14 we need to see that the Offerer is also the offering. We cannot separate the offering from the Offerer. Both are one. He Himself as the Offerer offered Himself as the offering, not through Himself but through the eternal Spirit. The

Spirit was the channel through whom Christ performed this excellent thing. The Spirit here is related to both His being and His doing. The act of offering is a doing, but the sacrifice itself is related to His being. The Spirit being eternal means that He is perfect, complete, short of nothing. *Eternal* implies everything. The eternal Spirit in Hebrews 9:14 includes both the essential and economical aspects of the Spirit.

Even in accomplishing redemption by offering Himself on the cross, the Lord Jesus did not act by Himself. He did it through the eternal Spirit, offering Himself without blemish to God the Father. Furthermore, He did not offer anything to Himself. Whatever He offered was to God, and whatever He did was to God. The issue of His offering is that His blood purifies our conscience from dead works so that we may serve the living God, the Triune God. The Lord did nothing by Himself, nothing to Himself, and nothing for Himself. Whatever He did was to God and for God.

Here again we can see the humility and the selflessness of the Son. We can also see the harmony in the Divine Trinity. The Son is the center of the Divine Trinity. We should not forget that the very central point of the Divine Trinity behaved Himself in such a way. He did not trust in Himself but in another One. Whatever He did was not for Himself but for the Father, and whatever issued out of Him went to the Father. He was altogether not by Himself, for Himself, or to Himself.

This is a good pattern that our Head has set up for His Body, of which we all are members. As members of Him, we should behave, act, and live according to what He did and was. When we do things, we should learn to do them not by ourselves. We are the doers, but we should not be the channel. We need someone else to be our channel through which we do things. Furthermore, we should not be the beneficiary of what we do. Someone else should be our beneficiary to receive the very benefit of our doing and of our being.

The move of the Divine Trinity as seen in Hebrews 9:14 and Matthew 12:28 is an excellent and beautiful example for us to follow. In saving us, He did not act individualistically. He did not do things to Himself and for Himself, nor did He trust in Himself. The New Testament record shows us such excellencies, beauties, and virtues in the Divine Trinity. There are so many beautiful items in this dear One. He humbled Himself to become a lowly man, even a slave. While He was on the earth as a slave, He acted in a way of not trusting Himself and not doing anything by Himself, to Himself, or for Himself. Eventually, God the Father highly exalted Him.

MATTHEW 28:19

In Matthew 28:19 the Lord charged His disciples to baptize people into the name of the Divine Trinity—the Father, the Son, and the Holy Spirit. At this point in Matthew the Triune God had been completed and consummated. For the Divine Trinity to be completed, to be consummated, He needed to go through a process to pick up humanity. If He had merely divinity, He would not be the consummated Triune God. To be the consummated Triune God, the completed Triune God, He needed humanity as well as divinity.

He also needed to pass through a beautiful, all-inclusive death. Death in Adam is ugly, terrible, and terrifying, but death in Christ is beautiful. We all have to be conformed to His dear death. The death of Christ is lovable and dear, and the Triune God needed it for His completion, for His consummation. The Divine Trinity is undoubtedly omnipotent, but if He were short of this beautiful death, He would not be able to solve our problems. In Him and with Him there is an all-inclusive death that can kill all the "germs" related to us. The Triune God is an all-inclusive dose within us with the killing element of the death of Christ. Within this all-inclusive dose there are many elements that can supply us in a positive way, and there is also the element of His death that can eliminate the negative things. The death of Christ on the cross took away all the "negative germs" in the universe. Such a death has been brought into the Divine Trinity. Praise the Lord for such an accomplished death!

After He had passed through the process of crucifixion, He entered into the realm of resurrection and became a life-giving Spirit. He then came back to His disciples in the atmosphere and reality of His resurrection to charge them to make the nations the kingdom people by baptizing them into the name, the person, the reality, of the Divine Trinity. Now that the Divine Trinity has been completed, consummated, people can be baptized into Him. The completed Triune God, the consummated Divine Trinity, is perfect, complete, and short of nothing. When we baptize people, we are placing them into the completed, consummated Triune God.

The name of the Triune God is a three-one name. This name is the Father, the Son, and the Spirit. The Father, the Son, and the Spirit is the name of the Divine Trinity into whom we baptize people. The Lord revealed this divine title in the context of His desire to put the people who have received our preaching into the Triune God. The Triune God in His divine trinity is the very place where we should put those who have received Him.

We go to disciple the nations, baptizing them. The word *disciple* is a strong word. A number of messages would be needed to explain this word thoroughly. The disciples were to disciple the unbelieving nations by baptizing them into the name of the Father and of the Son and of the Holy Spirit. This means that discipling includes baptizing. We have to disciple people by baptizing them, putting them into a person, the Triune God. When they get into this person, they are discipled. We should not preach the gospel to people without baptizing them. That is not scriptural. We should baptize people immediately after they have believed in the Lord. To disciple them by baptizing them is to make them the very citizens of the kingdom of the heavens. If we do not put them into the Triune God, we cannot bring them into the kingdom of God. We must put them into God Himself. Then we place them into the kingdom of God.

HEBREWS 2:3-4

Hebrews 2:3 and 4 also show us the Divine Trinity in His divine move. First, there is so great a salvation being spoken by the Lord [the Son]. Then God [God the Father] bears witness to the great salvation by signs and wonders and by various works of power and by distributions of the Holy Spirit. God's full salvation, so great a salvation, is wrapped up with the three of the Godhead. We may wonder why there are three in the Godhead and not one. If there were only one in the divine Godhead, there would be no beauty and no excellency. All the beauty, the excellency, the attributes, and the virtues found in the Godhead depend upon the divine Godhead being three yet one. Three yet one—here is the beauty; here is the excellency.

Likewise, in the corporate constitution of the Body of Christ, composed of millions of members, there is much beauty, excellency, and virtue. Millions of members have been composed together and constituted together to become members one of another. In this corporate constitution are many beauties, excellencies, virtues, and attributes. Eventually, all of these millions of members will be the constituents of the New Jerusalem, which will be the ultimate, corporate expression of the Triune God, full of beauty.

Suppose that in the church life there is a group of sisters and brothers who are serving and living in the reality of the Body of Christ. In their serving they are one and very harmonious. They are all humble. There is not one of them who is for himself, by himself, or to himself. In such a service in the Body, beauty and excellency are displayed. If there were thousands of saints on the earth living and serving in such a way, what beauty and excellency there would be! In the church life, in the Body life, in the new man, it is marvelous to see saints from every race and background meeting together in oneness. To have harmony in the church life requires humility and selflessness. The harmony in the church life is beautiful. This kind of beauty was first displayed in the Divine Trinity. The Divine Trinity took the lead to exhibit this kind of beauty in the universe. Among the three, the Son took the lead to be so selfless, so humble, and so considerate of the others.

LUKE 15:3-32

In Luke 15 there are three parables: the parable of a good shepherd finding a lost sheep, the parable of a fine woman seeking her lost coin, and the parable of a loving father receiving back his prodigal son (vv. 3-32). These three parables in Luke 15 give us a full picture of the Divine Trinity in saving lost sinners. First, there is the Son's finding (vv. 4-7) as the good Shepherd. The Son came to find us by accomplishing His all-inclusive redemption. Then there is the Spirit's seeking (vv. 8-10). The Spirit comes as the fine woman to do her seeking work. The Spirit enters into our heart to enlighten us, to search us, and to sweep away all the "dirt" in order to find us, to gain us. After being caught by the Spirit, we repent and come to ourselves (v. 17). Then we make up our mind to come back to the Father, typified by the prodigal son coming back to his father (vv. 18-24). The father, who was waiting for the prodigal son's return, saw his son and ran to him. He clothed him with the best robe, which typifies our Father clothing us with Christ as our righteousness. Then the father gave the command to kill the fattened calf for their enjoyment. This signifies the rich Christ (Eph. 3:8) killed on the cross for the believers' enjoyment. Luke 15 presents a full picture of the Divine Trinity in saving sinners by His divine love. Again we can see a marvelous coordination among the three of the Divine Trinity. These three—typified by a shepherd, a woman, and a father—cooperate together as one person in saving sinners.

EPHESIANS 2:18

Ephesians 2:18 speaks of our access through Christ [the Son] in one Spirit unto the Father. Why can we not come to the Father directly? Why do we have to approach the Father through Christ in the Spirit? We should not forget that the very God whom we are approaching is triune. As we have seen, none of the three in the Divine Trinity would be individualistic. If we would come to the Father without the Son and the Spirit, the Father would not be happy. The Father desires that we come to Him through the Son and in the Spirit. Through God the Son who is the Accomplisher, the means, and in God the Spirit who is the Executor, the application, we have access unto God the Father who is the Originator, the source of our enjoyment.

Again, we need to realize that the three of the Godhead are one. When They act, They act in oneness with one another. If we want to enjoy the Holy Spirit, we must love the Lord Jesus, the Son. When we say, "Lord Jesus, I love You," we enjoy the Spirit. Furthermore, when we tell the Lord that we love Him, the Lord would secretly impress us within to obey the Spirit and honor the Father. He would lead us to worship the Father. The Father is seeking those who will worship Him in the Son and through the Spirit. The Father always likes to exalt the Son, the Son always likes to honor the Father, and the Spirit always likes to testify for the Son with the Father.

Ephesians 2:18 tells us that if we come to approach God our Father, our access must be through the redeeming Son and in the guiding Spirit. Then we reach the loving Father. When we have the Father, we have the Son. When we have the Son with the Father, we have the Spirit. Therefore, we have the three of the Divine Trinity. We can never separate Them. The divine revelation of the divine economy shows us the Divine Trinity in all His excellencies, beauties, and virtues. These excellencies, beauties, and virtues are seen in the divine coordination in the Godhead.

TITUS 3:4-6

Titus 3:4-6 also reveals the Divine Trinity in the divine move and in our experience. These verses speak of the kindness and the love to man of our Savior God [God the Father] having appeared—God the Father having saved us. He saved us through the washing of regeneration and the renewing of the Holy Spirit, poured out upon us richly. This was through Jesus Christ [the Son] our Savior. This portion of the Word speaks of our Savior God and of Jesus Christ our Savior. These are not two Saviors but one Savior in two aspects. Our Savior God is Jesus Christ our Savior. Our salvation was carried out by God the Father, by God the Son, and by God the Spirit. With God the Father there was kindness and love to man. Furthermore, He poured out the Spirit upon us richly through Jesus Christ our Savior, God the Son. Then with the Spirit there is the washing of regeneration and the renewing. The salvation of the Triune God is a complete, entire, whole salvation. It includes the forgiveness of sins, redemption, justification, reconciliation, regeneration, and renewing. This renewing includes dispositional sanctification, transformation, conformation, and glorification. Our glorification will be the ultimate renewing. This is all carried out by the Divine Trinity in His divine move.

FIRST JOHN 4:13-14

First John 4:13 and 14 show that we are abiding in God [the Father] and He in us, that God the Father has given to us of His Spirit, and that the Father has sent the Son as the Savior of the world. Verse 13 says that God the Father has given to us "of" His Spirit. This means He has given us something of the Spirit, which indicates that all the riches of Christ are now the very content of the Spirit. Eventually, what God has given us is the complete, consummated, all-inclusive, compound, life-giving, indwelling processed Spirit. Our God, the Father, has given us of this all-inclusive Spirit, who is the bountiful supply of Jesus Christ, the Son.

GALATIANS 4:4-6

In Galatians 4:4-6 we see [the Triune] God sending forth His Son to redeem us under law that we might receive the sonship. We also see God [the Father] sending forth the Spirit of His Son into our hearts, crying, Abba, Father! The Father sent the Son to accomplish redemption for us so that we might have the sonship. This indicates that the Father's goal is to gain us for His sonship, and the Son's redemption is also for this. The Father also sent forth the Spirit of His Son. In the Triune God's salvation, the Son accomplished redemption for us on the cross. Now the Spirit of the Son is within us to bring us into the realization of the sonship. His redemption obtained the sonship, and now His indwelling Spirit is bringing us into the reality of the sonship. This is why we need two "sending forths" by the Father—the sending forth of the Son and the sending forth of the Spirit of the Son. God the Father sent forth God the Son to redeem us under law that we might receive the sonship. He also sent forth God the Spirit to impart His life into us that we might become His sons in reality. The Triune God is producing many sons for the fulfilling of His eternal purpose.

The Father as the source is the Sender. First, He sent forth the Son, and second, He sent forth the Spirit of the Son. We can see that the three in the Godhead are moving. The first One is the active One, sending forth. The second One is the sent One. The sent One has a third One as His Spirit. The three of the Godhead are not only omnipotent but also omnipresent. Therefore, the first One can send the second One and still be one with the second One. Furthermore, the first One can send the third One, and the third One is still one with the second One and the first One. This is the divine oneness in the Godhead. There is also a distinction among the three. All the beauties and all the excellencies exhibited by the Divine Trinity come from this distinction. There is a distinction among the Father, the Son, and the Spirit, yet the three are one.

ROMANS 8:9

Romans 8:9 speaks of the Spirit of God [the Father] dwelling in us and also speaks of the Spirit of Christ [the Son]. The Spirit of God and the Spirit of Christ are not two Spirits. They are one Spirit in two aspects. The Spirit of God is the Spirit of Christ. This indicates that God and Christ are one. God and Christ being one is shown by the fact that the Spirit is the Spirit of both God and Christ. God the Father, Christ the Son, and God the Spirit are in us. They are indwelling us, making Their home in us. We have a wonderful Occupant inside of us, a triune Occupant. Romans 8:9 shows us the beauty of the three of the Divine Trinity working together for our benefit.

FIRST CORINTHIANS 12:4-6

First Corinthians 12:4-6 speaks of the gifts of the same Spirit, the ministries of the same Lord [the Son], and the operations of the same God [God the Father], who is operating all things in all. The gifts are by the Spirit; the ministries, the services, are for the Lord; and the operations are of God. Ministries here simply mean services, the serving works. Here the Triune God is involved in these three things—gifts, ministries, and operations. The gifts by the Spirit are to carry out the ministries, the services, for the Lord, and the ministries for the Lord are to accomplish the operations, the works, of God. This is the Triune God moving in the believers for the accomplishment of His eternal purpose to build up the church, the Body of Christ, for the expression of God.

The gifts come from the Spirit, and they issue in the ministries, the services, of the Son. Furthermore, the ministries, the services, of the Son accomplish the operations, the works, of God the Father. This is the three-one God, operating, moving, and distributing His gifts among all of us. Here again we see the beauty, the harmony, and the excellency in the three working together. The Father operates, the Son ministers, and the Spirit gives the gifts. Furthermore, we are the beneficiaries, receiving all the benefits of the operating One, the ministering One, and the gift-giving One.

Eph 3: → outside of the self.

PORTIONS IN THE NEW TESTAMENT
REVEALING THE DIVINE TRINITY
IN THE DIVINE MOVE AND
IN OUR EXPERIENCE

(3)

Scripture Reading: Eph. 3:14-19; 4:4-6; 5:19-20; 6:10-11, 17; 1 John 4:2; 1 Pet. 4:14; 2 Cor. 13:14; Jude 20-21; 2 Thes. 2:13-14; Rev. 1:4-5; 22:1-2

In this chapter we want to continue our fellowship concerning portions in the New Testament revealing the Divine Trinity in the divine move and in our experience. Most of these portions are very deep. In Ephesians 3 Paul speaks of the breadth, length, height, and depth of Christ (v. 18). Our fellowship here concerning the Divine Trinity is in the direction of His depth.

EPHESIANS 3:14-19

Ephesians 3:14-19 reveals the apostle praying to the Father; the Father strengthening the believers through the Spirit; Christ making His home in the believers' hearts; and the believers being rooted and grounded in love, apprehending the dimensions of Christ, and knowing the knowledge-surpassing love of Christ to be filled unto all the fullness of [the Triune] God. In Ephesians 1 Paul prayed that God would give us a spirit of wisdom and revelation that we might know Him and His economy (v. 17). Paul prayed that we would have the ability, the power, to see the spiritual revelation. In chapter 1 his prayer is for our seeing the vision, but in chapter 3 his prayer is for our experience of the depths of Christ.

First, Paul prayed to the Father as the source. Then the Father strengthens the believers through the Spirit as the means, the channel. Then Christ moves and works to make His home in the believers' hearts. Eventually, the issue of the moving of the Father and the Spirit and the issue of the Son making His home in our hearts is the fullness of the Triune God. The Father is the source, the Spirit is the means, the Son is the object, and the fullness of the Triune God is the issue.

The source is the Father, the means is the Spirit, and the aim, the goal, is the Son because the Son is the center. Whatever the Triune God does is for the Son as the center, out of the Father as the source, and through the Spirit as the means. Paul prayed to the Father as the source, asking the Father to strengthen the believers through the channel of the Spirit that a goal might be reached. The goal was that Christ would make His home in the hearts of the believers.

Paul prayed to the Father, "of whom every family in the heavens and on earth is named" (3:15). The Father is the source, not only of us, the regenerated believers, the household of the faith (Gal. 6:10), but also of the God-created mankind (Luke 3:38), of the God-created Israel (Isa. 63:16; 64:8), and of the God-created angels (Job 1:6). In the heavens there is the angelic family. On the earth there is the family of mankind, the family of Israel, and the family of the faith. The Father is the source of these four families. To the family of the faith, the Father is not only the source as the creating One but also the source as the begetting One. The other three families have only the created life of God as their source, but we, as the family of the faith, have the divine life with the divine nature of God Himself. We have the Father's life with the Father's nature because the Triune God has entered into us. The apostle prayed that the Triune God's entering into us would be deeper; he prayed that the indwelling Christ might make His home, become fully settled, in our hearts. The thought of the apostle's prayer here is very deep.

Christ's making His home in the believers' hearts was initiated not by the Triune God but actually by the apostle Paul. The Triune God may be likened to a big machine, of which Paul was the operator. His prayer "turned the wheel." We have to learn

[Handwritten top margin: Allow the Lord to Calibrate our conscience.]

[Handwritten top margin: Lord, are You really bothered by this? I don't want to bother sth that's not bothered by You. Make home in our mind, emotion, will and conscience. Our conscience should function according to the sense of life. need to be clear, as well as to be pure. Our conscience functions according to the knowledge of truth.]

one lesson, that is, that there is a high principle in the entire universe. This principle is that God wants to do something, but He will only be the "machine," and He needs someone to be the operator. Today I hope that the church would be the operator. Whatever the apostle Paul did was done in a representing way. He was a representative of the entire Body of Christ. Now the operator of the universal "machine," the Triune God, is the church, the Body of Christ. But just because the church operates does not mean that the church in itself carries out. The church operates, but the "machine," the Triune God, carries out.

[Handwritten margin: We should allow Him to transform our conscience, so that He can lead our action according to Him.]

The Father, the Son, and the Spirit are the three "parts" of this universal "machine," and the Body is the operator. The Father is the source, the Spirit is the means, and the Son is the aim, the goal. According to Ephesians 3, the operator asks the "machine" to strengthen the operator through a channel. The Spirit as the channel does the work within us to strengthen every part of our being into the inner man so that the goal, the aim, the Son, might make His home within all the parts of our heart.

[Handwritten margin: Food sacrificed by to idol. not eat. Do all things for the building up. Ephesians 3]

The picture presented in Ephesians 3:14-19 again shows the very beautiful, fine, and deep coordination of the Triune God. The Father answers the operator's prayer. Then the Father works, not by Himself but by the third One, the Spirit, as the channel. Neither the Father nor the Spirit do something for Themselves. Both the source and the channel do something for the goal, the aim, the Son. Furthermore, the Son's making His home in all His believers' hearts is not for Himself. Each of the three does not act for Himself. Eventually, whatever They do is absolutely for the very fullness of the Triune God. This is a beautiful picture of the Divine Trinity in His deeper work within us. He works in a very complete and deep way to make His home in our hearts. Our hearts are composed of the mind, the emotion, and the will, plus the conscience of our spirit. Christ is making His home in these four parts by the preparation made through the channel, the Spirit, as an answer to the apostle's prayer made to the source, the Father. Eventually, the Son becomes settled in each part of our heart.

[Handwritten margin: Ephesians 4 One Body]

[Handwritten margin: Lord, this is from my inward parts, not Yours.]

[Handwritten margin: When someone is in trouble, we need help them, not to judge/criticize them.]

Whenever a person moves into a new house, it takes him a

[Handwritten bottom margin: Lord has put an "app" in us that translates the Word of God when we read His Word.]

while to become settled in that house. His getting settled is his making his home in the house. This is what Paul means by Christ making His home in our hearts. Christ wants to become settled in every part of our heart. Paul realized that the believers in Ephesus had Christ in them but that they did not have Christ making His home, getting Himself settled, in every part of their heart. This is why Paul prayed such a prayer. Our emotion, mind, will, and conscience must be touched by Christ and gained by Christ. The indwelling, occupying Christ needs to take over our emotion, our mind, our will, and our conscience until He gets Himself fully settled in all the inner rooms of our inner being. This is carried out in a coordinated way by the Divine Trinity. The three coordinate together in a beautiful way so that Christ, the embodiment of the Triune God, can become fully settled in our inner being.

While Christ is making His home in our hearts, we are rooted for growth and grounded for building. Christ making His home in our hearts is a matter in faith, not a matter of sensation. We must believe that today Christ as the very embodiment of the Triune God is settling Himself in our inner being. While He is doing this, we are rooted for growth and grounded for building in love.

Then we can apprehend with all the saints the dimensions of Christ—the breadth and the length and the height and the depth. In our experience of Christ, we first experience the breadth of what He is and then the length. This is horizontal. When we advance in Christ, we experience the height and depth of His riches. This is vertical. These are the dimensions of a cube. Our experience of Christ must be so rich, strong, perfect, and complete like a cube.

Then we will know the knowledge-surpassing love of Christ, issuing in the fullness of the Triune God. The fullness is the expression. If a cup is filled up with water until it is overflowing with water, the overflow of the water is an expression. That overflow is the fullness, and the fullness is the very expression of what is contained within the cup. When we experience Christ in such a deep way, this will issue in the fullness of the Triune God. This fullness is the church, the Body of Christ, as the very expression of the Triune God.

EPHESIANS 4:4-6

Ephesians 4:4 reveals that there is one Spirit for one Body with one hope. Without Paul's prayer in Ephesians 3, there would be no way for the believers to be one Body. Because the believers' inward parts have been taken over, occupied, by the settling Christ, the Spirit can be the very essence of the Body. The church as the Body of Christ has the Spirit as its essence with a hope. The hope is that the entire Body of Christ will be fully transfigured. Today much of our being still remains in the old creation, but we have a hope that one day the Lord will transfigure even our physical body into His likeness. Today the Spirit is the Body's essence. The Spirit as the essence of the Body needs to saturate our entire being until we are transfigured. We have a hope for this transfiguration.

Ephesians 4:5 speaks of one Lord [the Son] with one faith and one baptism. Faith united us to Christ in the organic union, and baptism cut us off, separated us, from the world. In other words, faith joins and baptism cuts. Now we are of the Lord because we have faith and baptism.

Verse 6 says that there is one God and Father of all—over all, through all, and in all. We need to be those who are enjoying the Father as the source of the Trinity. This One is in three directions. He is over all, through all, and in all. This means that the Father is triune. Actually, the Father is over all, the Son is through all, and the Spirit is in all. This shows that the Triune God is embodied in the Father who is also over all, through all, and in all.

EPHESIANS 5:19-20

Ephesians 5:19 and 20 also show the Divine Trinity in the divine move and in our experience. First, there is speaking to one another in psalms and hymns and spiritual songs [songs of the Spirit] in verse 19. The word *spiritual* shows that all the songs are spiritual poems of the Spirit. This means that the Spirit is the very essence of our psalms, hymns, and songs. The worldly poetry is of another kind of essence. When we sing our psalms, our hymns, and our songs, we have the deep feeling that we are touching another essence, and this essence is the very Spirit of God.

Verse 19b says that we should be singing and psalming with our heart to the Lord [the Son]. Our psalms, hymns, and spiritual songs are of the Spirit, but we sing them to the Lord, the Son. Then we need to be those giving thanks at all times for all things in the name of our Lord Jesus Christ to our God and Father (v. 20). We sing with the essence of the Spirit to the Son. Then we give thanks to the Father. All three of the Godhead are covered in Ephesians 5:19-20.

When we speak the psalms, the hymns, and the songs, we are speaking something of the essence of the Spirit. Then we render our singing, our psalming, to the Son, and we thank our Father in the name of the Son with the essence of the Spirit. This is our enjoyment of the Divine Trinity. However, very few Christians realize that whenever we sing or speak a hymn, we are enjoying the three of the Divine Trinity. We enjoy the essence of the Spirit, we enjoy the Lord as our goal, and we enjoy the Father as our object. We thank the Father and we sing songs to the Son with something of the essence of the Spirit. This is the way in which we enjoy the Triune God.

EPHESIANS 6:10-11, 17

All six chapters of the book of Ephesians are constructed with the Triune God. In Ephesians 6 the Divine Trinity is moving for the defeating of His enemy, for dealing with His opponent. For the Triune God to defeat His enemy, we need to be empowered in the Lord [the Son] and in the might of His strength (v. 10). Then we need to put on the whole armor of God [the Father] so that we may be able to stand against the stratagems of the devil (v. 11). Finally, verse 17 says that we need to receive the sword of the Spirit, which [the Spirit] is the word of God [the Father]. Through the Divine Trinity we receive the power and strength, we have the armor, and we also have the sword. If we did not have the power or the strength, we could not fight. For this we need to trust in the Son. We also need a covering to protect us. This is the armor, and the armor is of the Father. Then we need an offensive weapon against the enemy. This is the Spirit as the sword. The Son is the power and the strength for our fighting, the Father's armor is our covering, and the Spirit's sword is our offensive power. This shows that even in the spiritual warfare, we need the Divine Trinity.

FIRST JOHN 4:2

In 1 John 4:2 we can again see the coordination of the Divine Trinity. This verse shows us the Spirit of God [the Triune God including the Father], confessing Jesus Christ [the Son], being out of God [the Triune God]. The Spirit is not independent. He is of Someone, of God the Father. Furthermore, He does something, not for Himself but for the Son. He confesses Jesus Christ, the Son. Again we see the three working together for one goal—to exalt the Son as the very embodiment of the Triune God.

FIRST PETER 4:14

First Peter 4:14 says, "If you are reproached in the name of Christ, you are blessed, because the Spirit of glory and of God rests upon you." When we are reproached in the name of Christ [the Son], we are blessed. We are blessed because the Spirit of glory and of God [God the Father] rests upon us. Even in the persecution of the believers the three of the Divine Trinity are fully involved. They are wrapped up with the persecuted believers. When the believers of the Son are reproached, the Triune God is enjoying His rest by staying with them in their persecution. The Spirit of glory and of God the Father is resting upon the believers. *Resting* in this verse is a kind of staying, abiding, comforting, sustaining, covering, and protecting. While the Spirit of glory is staying with us, the suffering ones, He becomes our sustaining power, our protection, our covering, and our victory, yet with Him it is a resting. This explains the real situation of Christian persecution. When we are being persecuted, our Triune God is covering us, protecting us, sustaining us, and comforting us. He is resting upon us.

SECOND CORINTHIANS 13:14

Second Corinthians 13:14 speaks of the grace of the Lord Jesus Christ [the Son] and the love of God [the Father] and the fellowship of the Holy Spirit being with us all. The love of God is the source, since God is the origin; the grace of the Lord is the course of the love of God, since the Lord is the expression of God; and the fellowship of the Spirit is the impartation of the grace of the Lord with the love of God, since the Spirit is the transmission of the Lord with God, for our experience and enjoyment of the Triune God—the Father, the Son, and the Spirit.

JUDE 20-21

Jude 20 and 21 may be considered as a "sister" portion to 2 Corinthians 13:14. These verses say that we believers should be those praying in the Holy Spirit, keeping ourselves in the love of God [God the Father], and awaiting the mercy of our Lord Jesus Christ [the Son] unto eternal life [the life of the Triune God]. Praying in the Holy Spirit equals the fellowship of the Spirit in 2 Corinthians 13:14; keeping ourselves in the love of God is parallel with the love of God in that verse; and the mercy of our Lord Jesus Christ goes with the grace of Christ. Mercy and grace go together, but mercy goes farther and deeper to reach what grace cannot reach. God's mercy reaches farther than His grace. Mercy is for persons who are in a miserable and pitiful situation and condition. When the prodigal son came to his father in Luke 15, he was altogether in a miserable and pitiful condition. Whatever the father did for this pitiful, prodigal son was a mercy to him. Mercy is mentioned instead of grace in Jude 20 and 21 due to the church's degradation and apostasy. In the degraded situation of the churches God's mercy is needed. When the churches are in degradation, what they need is the Lord's far-reaching mercy.

We are awaiting the mercy of our Lord. The word *awaiting* implies trusting. While we await and look for the mercy of our Lord, we are also trusting in His mercy. We need to await the mercy of our Lord Jesus Christ unto eternal life. The enjoyment and inheritance of eternal life, the life of God, is the goal of our spiritual seeking. In these verses the three of the Trinity are involved in the believers' daily Christian life. The entire blessed Trinity is employed and enjoyed by the believers in their praying in the Holy Spirit, keeping themselves in the love of God the Father, and awaiting the mercy of our Lord, the Son, unto eternal life.

SECOND THESSALONIANS 2:13-14

Second Thessalonians 2:13 and 14 say, "We ought to thank God always concerning you, brothers beloved of the Lord, because God chose you from the beginning unto salvation in sanctification of the Spirit and belief of the truth, to which also He called you through our gospel unto the obtaining of the glory of our Lord Jesus Christ." God [God the Father] chose us from the beginning. This refers to eternity past. His salvation is in sanctification of the Spirit.

Sanctification in verse 13 is all-inclusive. It covers all three stages of sanctification. The first stage of sanctification is for our repentance and is mentioned in 1 Peter 1:2. First, we were foreknown by God the Father for His choosing. Then according to what God chose, the Holy Spirit came to us to separate us, to sanctify us from the world, from sin, and from all the sinners unto God. Through that kind of sanctifying, we repented and returned to God. This is the first stage of sanctification for our repentance.

The second stage of sanctification is for our justification. In the second stage the sanctification that we receive in God's full salvation is both positional and dispositional. Positional sanctification is mentioned in Hebrews 13:12, which says that Jesus sanctified us through His own blood. Positional sanctification is obtained by us through Christ's redeeming blood shed on the cross. Once we are bought back by the Lord's blood, we are separated from the world, receiving a sanctified position and being made holy unto Him. Furthermore, when we were saved and justified, we entered into an organic union with the Lord, partook of His divine life and nature, and were sanctified dispositionally (1 Cor. 6:11).

The third stage of sanctification for our transformation is mainly a dispositional sanctification. This is the very sanctification stressed in Romans 6:19 and 22. This sanctification takes place in our disposition, changing our very nature. This is for our transformation and also includes our conformation and glorification. Glorification is actually the last step, the ultimate step, of the Holy Spirit's sanctification. In this all-inclusive sanctification God's complete salvation is carried out.

Salvation in sanctification of the Spirit is the procedure, and the obtaining of the glory of our Lord Jesus Christ, the Son, is the goal. God's choosing and the Holy Spirit's sanctification, which carries out God's salvation, will have a result. This result will be the obtaining of the glory of the Lord Jesus Christ. This is our glorification. Again we see the three of the Divine Trinity involved with us from eternity past to eternity future. God's choosing was in eternity past, and God's glorification for us will be for eternity future. His all-inclusive salvation is from eternity to eternity.

REVELATION 1:4-5

Revelation 1:4 and 5 say, "Grace to you and peace from Him [the Triune God including the Father] who is and who was and who is coming, and from the seven Spirits who are before His throne, and from Jesus Christ [the Son], the faithful Witness, the Firstborn of the dead, and the Ruler of the kings of the earth." The Father is the One who is and who was and who is coming. He was in the past, He is in the present, and He is coming in the future. The seven Spirits who are before God's throne are the operating Spirit of God, God the Spirit. In person the Spirit is one, but in function He is seven. Some people have a three-way lamp, but the Spirit is a "seven-way lamp." God made His Spirit sevenfold intensified. The sevenfold intensified Spirit of God is needed for God's move and work on the earth.

Jesus Christ, as the faithful Witness, the Firstborn of the dead, and the Ruler of the kings of the earth, is God the Son. His being the faithful Witness refers to His earthly life of thirty-three and a half years. He was the Witness, the testimony, the expression, of God. His being the Firstborn of the dead refers to His resurrection. First, He lived on this earth as the faithful Witness. Then He resurrected from the dead to become the Firstborn of the dead for the church, the new creation. Today He is the Ruler of the kings of the earth in His ascension. He is ruling over the earth. He was living on this earth as the faithful Witness, then He rose up from the dead as the Firstborn of the dead, and now He is ruling over the earth, the entire world, as the Ruler of the kings of the earth. Thus, Revelation 1:4 and 5 show us that the Father is the One who is and who was and who is coming; the Spirit is the One who is intensified seven-fold; and the Son is the faithful Witness, the Firstborn of the dead, and the Ruler of the kings of the earth. From such a Triune God, grace and peace are imparted to the churches.

REVELATION 22:1-2

In Revelation 22:1 and 2 there is a river of water of life [the Spirit] proceeding out of the throne of God [the Triune God including the Father] and of the Lamb [the Son], and on the two sides of the river there is the tree of life [Christ the Son]. This is the wonderful picture presented at the end of the Bible. God's throne is the center of the holy city. Out of the throne proceeds a river of water of life, and along the two sides of this river grows the tree of life. The one tree of life growing on the two sides of the river signifies that the tree of life is a vine spreading and proceeding along the flow of the water of life for God's people to receive and enjoy. This is a marvelous sign in the book of Revelation, which is a book of signs.

The throne of God is the very center of the divine administration in the entire universe. Out of the throne proceeds the flow of the Spirit, the river of water of life. This is why the Spirit is referred to as the Spirit of life in Romans 8:2. The Spirit of life is the river of water of life. In this water of life Christ grows as the very life supply. Thus, we see God the Father as the source in His administration, God the Spirit in His flow as the water of life, and God the Son growing in the water of life as the tree of life to supply the entire city. The water saturates, and the tree supplies so that the entire city will live forever to express the Divine Trinity.

PORTIONS IN THE NEW TESTAMENT REVEALING THE DIVINE TRINITY IN THE DIVINE MOVE AND IN OUR EXPERIENCE

(4)

Scripture Reading: Matt. 3:16-17; Acts 2:32-33; Rom. 5:5-6; 2 Cor. 1:21-22; 5:5-6; Rom. 15:16; 2 Cor. 3:3; John 4:10; 1 John 5:6-9; Rev. 4:2—5:6; 1 Cor. 3:10-16; 1 Thes. 1:4-7

In this chapter we want to continue our fellowship concerning the portions in the New Testament revealing the Divine Trinity in the divine move and in our experience.

MATTHEW 3:16-17

Matthew 3:16 and 17 reveal the Divine Trinity in His divine move. These verses show Jesus standing in the baptizing water, the Spirit of God descending like a dove and coming upon Jesus [the Son], and the Father speaking out of the heavens, saying, "This is My Son, the Beloved, in whom I have found delight." The Spirit of God descending like a dove and coming upon Christ can be considered as God's anointing Him to be His Messiah to carry out His eternal purpose. This was an anointing to confirm God's appointing of His Son to be the very Christ to come to carry out God's economy. God's appointing of Christ transpired before the foundation of the world. In eternity past God appointed the Son to be His Christ, His Messiah, to carry out what God planned to do for His eternal purpose. Then Christ was incarnated, and this incarnated One passed through human living on earth. When He was thirty years of age, He came out to be baptized by John. At this juncture God anointed Him with the consummation of the Triune God as the anointing oil.

In ancient times the kings and the priests needed to be anointed to take their offices. The anointing is the confirmation of the appointing. The appointed Christ was in the water under an open heaven and was anointed by the Triune God with the economical Spirit. By that time Jesus had already been born of the essential Spirit. Before the Spirit of God descended and came upon Him, the Lord Jesus was born of the Spirit (Luke 1:35), proving that He already had the Spirit of God within Him. That was for His birth. Now for His ministry the Spirit of God descended upon Him. This was the fulfillment of Isaiah 61:1; 42:1; and Psalm 45:7 to anoint the new King and introduce Him to His people. He was conceived with the essential Spirit for His birth in order for Him to be a God-man to exist on the earth. Thirty years later He was baptized by John. While He was standing in the waters of baptism, God came to anoint Him with the Holy Spirit as the economical Spirit to carry out God's economy.

ACTS 2:32-33

Acts 2:32 and 33 reveal [the Triune] God having raised up Jesus [the Son], Jesus having been exalted to the right hand of God [the Father], and Jesus having received the Holy Spirit from the Father. This portion of the Word shows us the Divine Trinity in His divine move for His New Testament economy after Christ's ascension. The receiving of the Spirit by the Son from the Father was the beginning of the operation of God's New Testament economy. Through this receiving, the work of God for His New Testament economy began.

ROMANS 5:5-6

Romans 5:5 and 6 show the love of God [God the Father] having been poured out in our hearts through the Holy Spirit given to us and Christ [the Son] having died for the ungodly. The pouring out of God's love was carried out through the Holy Spirit, whom God has given to us. God has given the Holy Spirit to us, and through this Holy Spirit God's love has been poured out in our hearts. Furthermore, Christ [the Son] died for us, the ungodly. First, the Son died for us, the ungodly. Based upon this the Spirit was given to us, and through this Spirit given to us, the love of God has been poured out in our hearts. Now we enjoy the love of God through the Holy Spirit given to us on the foundation of the death of Christ for us, the ungodly.

SECOND CORINTHIANS 1:21-22

Second Corinthians 1:21 and 22 reveal that [the Triune] God has attached us unto Christ [the Son] and anointed us. These verses also show God having sealed us and having given the pledge of the Spirit in our hearts. First, God anointed the Son in the Jordan River. Then the believers were anointed by God. Our being anointed is a continuation of the anointing of Jesus. Actually, God has only one anointing, and this anointing is the anointing of Christ. In His resurrection the personal Christ, the individual Christ, was expanded, extended, increased, into the corporate Christ. The personal Christ is just Jesus Christ as the Head. As the Head, He was anointed when He was thirty years of age. But after His resurrection this personal Christ was expanded, extended, increased, to be the Body of Christ, the corporate Christ. This corporate Christ includes Jesus Christ as the Head and all His members as the Body. The Head was anointed first, and the Body was anointed later, but these should not be considered as two anointings. Actually, they are two steps of the same anointing. Eventually, we must say that God has anointed "the Christ," the corporate Christ, to carry out His New Testament economy. This corporate Christ includes both the Head and the Body.

The Lord Jesus, as the Head of this corporate Christ, was anointed at His baptism in the Jordan River. The Body of this corporate Christ was anointed on the day of Pentecost and in the house of Cornelius. In the entire universe there is only one anointing, and the anointing of the corporate Christ took place in two stages. All the anointings in the Old Testament are types. Aaron was anointed by Moses, and David was anointed by Samuel. All the kings and priests were anointed. They are types pointing to the unique anointing. This unique anointing covered the corporate Christ as the Head and the Body. All the Jewish believers were anointed on the day of Pentecost (Acts 1:5; 2:4), and all the Gentile believers were anointed in the house of Cornelius (10:44-47; 11:15-17). All of us believers were anointed to be the corporate Christ for the purpose of carrying out God's New Testament economy. We are the partners of the individual Christ (Heb. 3:14a). We are partners with Christ in a divine corporation. This divine corporation is "Christ and the church, incorporated." We are not employees in this corporation but partners with Christ. This is a great universal corporation to carry out God's eternal purpose. As the corporate Christ, we are the partners of Christ, cooperating with Him to carry out God's New Testament economy.

The Triune God has firmly attached us unto Christ. He has attached every member of the corporate Christ to the individual Christ. He has anointed us and has made us one with the Head. We have been attached to Christ by the organic connection through the anointing oil. The anointing oil is the consummated Spirit as the consummated Triune God. He is the compound, all-inclusive, life-giving, indwelling, sevenfold intensified, and processed Spirit. By such a Spirit we all have been attached unto Christ, the Head. We are the corporate Christ to carry out God's great and universal will, to carry out God's economy to build up the Body of Christ in an organic way.

For this purpose God has also sealed us and given the pledge of the Spirit in our hearts. The anointing is the sealing. Since God has anointed us with Christ, He has also sealed us in Him. The pledge of the Spirit is the Spirit Himself as the pledge. Sealing is a mark that we are God's inheritance, God's possession, belonging to God. The pledge is a guarantee that God is our inheritance, or heritage, belonging to us. The Spirit within us is the pledge, the earnest, of God being our portion in Christ.

Paul wrote his second Epistle to the Corinthians based upon this revelation of the Triune God. The Father has anointed His sons and attached them to their big Brother, the firstborn Son of God. The firstborn Son is the Head of the corporate Christ, and the many sons are the Body of the corporate Christ. By God the Father's anointing and attaching, He has made all His sons one with His Firstborn to be a corporate Body to carry out His eternal purpose. For His purpose the Father has sealed us and given us the sealing Spirit as an inward pledge to guarantee that God is our inheritance.

SECOND CORINTHIANS 5:5-6

Second Corinthians 5:5 and 6 show [the Triune] God having wrought us for our transfiguration; the Spirit having been given to us as a pledge; and us, at home in the body, being abroad from the Lord [the Son]. The word *wrought* is a difficult word to define. God has wrought us for our transfiguration. The word *wrought* means "fashioned, shaped, prepared, or made fit." God has wrought, fashioned, shaped, prepared, made us fit, for the very purpose that our mortal body might be swallowed up by His resurrection life. This will be our transfiguration. The word for *wrought* in the Chinese translation means to sow a seed into the soil and to water it that the seed may grow up to be a plant to blossom and to bear fruit. In order for the seed to fulfill its purpose of blossoming and bearing fruit, I have to work on it. First, I put it into the soil. Then I water it so that it can grow. This makes it prepared to be in a proper form so that it can carry out my purpose. In like manner God has wrought us for our transfiguration.

When we repented, believed in the Lord, and called upon His name, we were regenerated. The Triune God was put into us. From the moment we were regenerated, God began to fashion us, to work us. God wants to use us to fulfill His purpose. This is why we are still under God's working, God's fashioning, God's shaping. We will be under God's working until the day that we will be fully matured. The apostle Paul was eventually matured and ready to be transfigured. We need to allow God to work us until our mortal body is swallowed up by His resurrection life. God needs to work us, to prepare us, to fashion us, and to fit us for His purpose.

To work a piece of metal is to shape it by hammering it with tools. Then the metal is wrought. However, there is nothing organic about working a piece of metal. God's working us is fully organic. To sow something is organic. Watering helps this organic seed to grow as it gains the increase of the inner life. A piece of iron can be shaped and formed, but that is not organic. God's shaping us is organic by the growth in life. He shapes us by transforming us with the element of life. A piece of iron cannot be transformed. We can change its form, but that change is not transformation. Transformation is not merely an outward change but a change from within metabolically and organically. As the divine life grows and increases within us, we are transformed inwardly and organically. God is working us with Himself as the organic element added into our being that we may be transformed, not only in form but also in nature metabolically and organically. His divine life is added into our being, and His life element is changing us as it is increasing within us. Then we will be shaped, formed, and fitted so that we can be transfigured.

Different fruits have different kinds of shapes. An apple, a banana, and a coconut all have different shapes. The shapes of such fruits are not arrived at by outward regulation. We do not need to make a round box to shape an apple. Instead, as the life of the apple grows, it spontaneously becomes formed into its life shape. When we plant a seed and water it, the life within it grows. Eventually, the life's growing shapes the fruit into a certain kind of appearance. Therefore, the shape, the form, comes into being, not by outward regulation, such as hammering, but by the inward growing with the life element. Each kind of fruit has its own shape according to the very essence of its element. Similarly, we have the divine life, and this divine life has its own shape.

In 2 Corinthians 5:5 and 6 Paul's thought is that we were made in the image of God, and God has added Himself into our being as a growing element. Now God is working us so that we may grow. The growing of this divine life within us will shape us into a certain form that fits our coming transfiguration. The teaching of 2 Corinthians is altogether a shaping teaching, a forming teaching, a working teaching. God is working us to shape us, to form us, so that we may be fit for the upcoming transfiguration. Today we are here under His shaping, His working.

The entire book of 2 Corinthians is a "working book." God is working us all day by day throughout our entire lives. He is working us in the same way that a farmer works a little plant day by day. Eventually, the plant blossoms and bears fruit. The Triune God has wrought us for our transfiguration. At our transfiguration our entire being will be saturated with Christ. God has given us the Spirit as the pledge, the earnest, the foretaste, the guarantee, of this wonderful and marvelous part of His complete salvation for us in Christ. The pledge guarantees us that we will be transfigured. We will be transfigured by resurrection life swallowing the death in our mortal body (1 Cor. 15:54). Actually, our new body will be our old body that has been transfigured with the divine element under the divine working.

Presently, we are at home in the body and abroad from the Lord, the Son, until the day when He returns and we are raptured to meet Him. Then we will all be home together with Him. Our home is the Triune God (Psa. 90:1). By the divine element of the Triune God, we have been regenerated. We are now growing day by day with this divine element. Eventually, this divine element, which is actually the Triune God Himself, will be our eternal dwelling place in our transfiguration.

ROMANS 15:16

In Romans 15:16 Paul says that he is a minister of Christ Jesus [the Son] to the Gentiles, ministering as a laboring priest of the gospel of [the Triune] God, that the offering of the Gentiles might be acceptable, having been sanctified in the Holy Spirit. Paul was a priest of the gospel of the Triune God, ministering Christ Jesus, the Son, to the Gentiles. Eventually, the result of his work was to offer the Gentiles to God as a sanctified entity through the Holy Spirit.

SECOND CORINTHIANS 3:3

In 2 Corinthians 3:3 Paul tells the Corinthians that they are a letter of Christ [the Son], ministered by the apostles, inscribed not with ink but with the Spirit of the living God [the Triune God]. Here again we can see the Divine Trinity in the divine move and in our experience. Eventually, the believers become a letter to communicate the Son, and this letter is written with the Spirit as the ink. This Spirit is the very element of the living God, the Triune God, for writing this letter that conveys Christ.

JOHN 4:10

In John 4:10 the Lord Jesus told the Samaritan woman, "If you knew the gift of God and who it is who says to you, Give Me a drink, you would have asked Him, and He would have given

you living water." In this verse we see the gift of God [God the
Father] and the Son as the Giver of the living water [the Spirit].
Even in such a short verse we can see the three of the Divine
Trinity. The Father is the Possessor of the gift, the Son is the
Giver of the gift, and the Spirit is the gift. The entire New Tes-
tament speaks concerning the Divine Trinity with different
expressions and from different angles.

FIRST JOHN 5:6-9

In 1 John 5:6-9 we are told that the Spirit, as the reality,
testifies (v. 6) that the testimony of God [the Father] is greater
than the testimony of men (v. 9a) and that God has testified
concerning His Son (v. 9b). All three of the Divine Trinity are
involved in this testifying. The Spirit testifies, His testifying is
the Father's testimony, and the Father's testimony is concerning the Son.

REVELATION 4:2—5:6

Revelation 4:2—5:6 is a record of a universal scene. In this
scene there is God [the Triune God] sitting on the throne (4:2),
the seven Spirits of God and the seven lamps of fire burning
before the throne of God (v. 5), and the Lamb standing in the
midst of the throne and of the four living creatures and elders
(5:6). The throne of the Triune God is the center. In front of this
throne are seven burning lamps, which are the seven Spirits
of God. In the midst of the throne and of the four living creatures
and in the midst of the elders is a Lamb standing. The Father,
the Son, and the Spirit are moving in this scene to carry out the
eternal economy of the Triune God. His economy was a mystery. No one in the universe was qualified to open this mystery
except the slain Lamb. He has the qualifications and the standing to open the scroll, to open the mystery of the universe, the
mystery of God's economy.

FIRST CORINTHIANS 3:10-16

In 1 Corinthians 3:10-16 Paul speaks of the grace of God
[the Triune God] given to him (v. 10), the foundation laid being
[the Son] Jesus Christ (v. 11), and the Spirit of God dwelling in
us as the temple of God (v. 16). This portion of the Word describes

how the church comes into being and how the church exists. It shows the move of the Divine Trinity to have the church for His corporate expression.

FIRST THESSALONIANS 1:4-7

In 1 Thessalonians 1:4-7 Paul tells the believers that they are beloved of God [the Father], that the gospel came to them in power and in the Holy Spirit and with the joy of the Holy Spirit so that they became imitators of the Lord [the Son]. After we have received the gospel in the power of the Spirit and with the joy of the Spirit, we become imitators of the Lord. This portion shows the activity of the Divine Trinity in the service of the gospel.

All the portions in the New Testament that we have pointed out should give us a clear view that the New Testament is fully composed of and structured with the Divine Trinity. The Bible presents us a picture of the move of the Divine Trinity for the accomplishment of His economy that we might be wrought to fit His economy.

LIVING IN THE DIVINE TRINITY

(1)

Scripture Reading: 1 Pet. 1:2; Acts 13:39; Rom. 3:24; John 1:12-13; 3:6b, 15; Eph. 1:13; John 15:5; 1 John 2:6, 24; 3:24; 2:27

In this chapter and in the following chapters, we want to see the practical experience of living in and with the Divine Trinity. The Lord Jesus told us in John 15 that He is the vine and that we are the branches of the vine. As the branches of the vine, we should abide in Him. Then He will abide in us. To abide in Christ is to live in Christ, and to live in Christ is to live in the Divine Trinity. To have Christ abide in us is to have the Triune God living in us. This is to live with the Divine Trinity. Therefore, to abide in Christ is to live in the Divine Trinity, and to have Christ abiding in us is to live with the Divine Trinity. The book of John is a book on living in and with the Divine Trinity. The truth concerning living in and with the Divine Trinity is greatly expounded in the Epistles, especially in those written by Paul. In the Epistles we can see all the practicalities and details of living in and with the Divine Trinity. We need to be brought into the experiences of living in the Divine Trinity and with the Divine Trinity. When we abide in Him, we live in Him. When we have Him abide in us, we live with Him. *We need to abide in Him before He can live in us.*

THE BELIEVERS' INITIAL EXPERIENCE OF THE DIVINE TRINITY

To see our living in and with the Divine Trinity, we have to know, to realize, and to apprehend our initial experience of the Divine Trinity. Anything that is in the initial stage is a foundation.

Sanctified by the Spirit

We have a foundation as a strong base for us to have a life of living in the Divine Trinity and with the Divine Trinity. The sanctification by the Spirit is the very start of our initial experience of the Triune God (1 Pet. 1:2). This corresponds with our experience. We were chosen before the foundation of the world (Eph. 1:4). Our being chosen transpired in eternity past. Then in time God called us. God's calling is implied in our being sanctified by the Spirit.

Before we were saved, we were wandering without any meaning or purpose. Somehow we were able to hear the preaching of the gospel. Actually, this preaching was a sounding of God's call. When we go out to visit people to preach the gospel to them, this can be considered as a kind of calling to them. However, merely our preaching alone cannot constitute God's calling. God's calling includes our preaching plus the sanctification of the Spirit.

When we go out to preach the gospel, we are sounding the trumpet of God's call. Furthermore, the sanctifying, the separating, and the seeking Spirit cooperates with us. We are preaching, and He is seeking. We are preaching, and He is separating. We are preaching, and He is sanctifying. Then our candidates repent, and their repentance is an answer to the sounding of God's call. Their repentance comes out of the Spirit's separation. The work of the Spirit is a seeking work, a separating work, and a sanctifying work. Our preaching plus the Spirit's separating is the call, and the people's repentance is the answer to the call.

This is fully portrayed in Luke 15. In Luke 15 there is a parable of a fine woman seeking a lost coin. She did a fine work by enlightening the room and searching everywhere. Due to the enlightening and searching of the Spirit depicted by this fine woman, the prodigal son in the following parable came to himself. Verses 17 and 18a say, "When he came to himself, he said, How many of my father's hired servants abound in bread, but I am perishing here in famine! I will rise up and go to my father." His being awakened was the issue of the Spirit's fine seeking and the Spirit's finding. Due to the Spirit's fine seeking, the prodigal son woke up and made up his mind to return to his father. The Spirit's enlightening, searching, and seeking brought him to repentance. Although this happened to him, I do not think that the prodigal son knew that this was due to the Spirit's sanctifying work. It was the same with us in our experience. We did not realize that our repentance was the issue of the Holy Spirit's sanctifying work. Unconsciously, we experienced the sanctifying Spirit of the Divine Trinity.

I was born into Christianity and was raised in it for at least nineteen years. During that time I had not received the Lord Jesus. One day out of curiosity I went to listen to a young lady preaching the gospel. In that meeting I was caught by the Lord. No doubt, the Holy Spirit was working on me, seeking me out, separating me, and sanctifying me. The message that I heard was concerning the type of the children of Israel enjoying Christ as their passover and passing through the Red Sea into the wilderness to escape the usurping hand of Pharaoh, who typifies Satan. As a result of this word, I declared that I wanted to go out of the world and not be under the usurping hand of the evil one, Satan, any longer. All of us who are regenerated Christians have experienced the Spirit's sanctifying work in this way. This is the first step, our initial experience of the Triune God.

Justified through the Redemption of Christ

Following this sanctifying work, we were justified through the redemption of Christ (Acts 13:39; Rom. 3:24). After repenting, we did not know much about Christ, but we began to treasure Him, to appreciate Him. We began to have a good feeling about Him, even though no one had said much about Him to us. We had such an inner feeling. Spontaneously, some of us might have said, "I love Jesus. Jesus is very good." This is a sign that we have believed in Him and that He has redeemed us. God the Father justified us, and this justification implies reconciliation. It also implies God's willing acceptance. We have been brought into peace with our God. Our sins have been forgiven, and all our sinfulness has been washed away. We have been forgiven, washed, reconciled, justified, and accepted through Christ's redemption.

Born of God through the Regeneration of the Spirit with the Divine Life

We were also born of God through the regeneration of the Spirit with the divine life (John 1:12-13; 3:6b, 15). Following God's forgiveness, God's washing, God's reconciliation, God's justification, and God's willing acceptance of us through Jesus' redemption, the Holy Spirit enlivened our dead spirit. Then we were born of God.

Sealed with the Spirit

Furthermore, we were sealed with the Spirit (Eph. 1:13). The Spirit was put upon us as a living seal. This was our initial experience of the Triune God. We can even say that this was our enrollment into the experience of the Triune God.

LIVING IN THE DIVINE TRINITY— ABIDING IN CHRIST AS THE TRUE VINE

Not about self-improving in any other religions, but we can live in Him, and He can live in us

Now we want to see what it means to live in the Divine Trinity. Outside of the divine revelation of the Bible, there is no religion or philosophy that says that we can live in another person. But the Bible reveals that we can live in the Triune God. What a wonder and an honor it is to be those who can live in the Triune God! To live in the Triune God is miraculous. In the entire universe there is such a miracle that we can live in the Triune God.

a branch doesn't abide in the vine one day in a week. (LD- going to the church).

To live in the Divine Trinity is to abide in Christ as the true vine (John 15:5). Christ likened Himself to a vine tree. The illustration of a vine tree gives us the proper understanding of what it means to be in Him. The branches are abiding in the vine tree. This means that the branches are living in the tree. To live in the Triune God is just like the branches abiding in a vine tree. It is wonderful that Christ as the embodiment of the Triune God is a vine tree. Jesus is not a pine tree but a vine tree spreading and growing over the entire earth. His fruit is so available to us because He is the vine tree.

This vine tree has many branches. All the branches are the completion of the tree. Without its branches a vine tree would not be a complete tree. This tree with all its branches is an organism to express its inner life and to fulfill its purpose. God *we first needs to be organically connected to Him through regeneration. we can be part of His organism.*

with His divine life needs some expression, and He has a purpose. Because of this He needs an organism to express His life and to fulfill His purpose. Christ is this organism, the vine tree, and now we are abiding in Him.

The Greek word for *abide* means not only to remain or to stay but also to have our home, or to make our home. In John 14 the same word is used as a noun. The Lord told us that in His Father's house there are many abodes (v. 2) and that He would come to make an abode with His lovers (v. 23). An abode is a dwelling place. Therefore, to abide is to dwell in a home. To live in Christ as the embodiment of the Triune God means that we take Christ as our dwelling place for our daily life. As long as the branches abide in the tree, they have their daily life in the tree because they are living there. Now we should understand the real denotation of living in the Triune God. To live in the Triune God is to have Him as our dwelling place, as our home, for our daily life. The vine tree with its branches is the very organism of the Triune God. Thus, to live in the Triune God is to abide in Christ as God's organism.

Abiding in the Lord

We need to be those abiding in the Lord (1 John 2:6). To abide in the Triune God is to abide in the Lord. The Lord is the One who possesses all things, who rules over all things, who exercises His sovereignty over all things and over all people. We are living in the One who is the Lord of this universe. If we are not obedient to Him or do not subject ourselves to Him, that will annul our abiding in Him. To abide in Christ is to abide in the Lord.

To abide in the vine tree implies a daily life. We need to consider the branches of the vine tree. They are having their "daily life" in the vine tree. We need to have our daily life in the Lord. This means that we have to obey Him and that we have to walk in the same way that He walked. As a man, He walked under God's authority. We also need to walk under His authority, submitting ourselves to Him.

Abiding in the Son

We also need to be those abiding in the Son (v. 24b). In the New Testament the Son is the One who possesses the Father's life with the Father's nature to express the Father. The sons have the full right to enjoy all the privileges and rights ascribed to the sonship. When we are abiding in the Son, we enjoy our Father's life, our Father's nature, and the privilege, the right, to express Him and to enjoy all His possessions. To abide in the Lord concerns the lordship of Christ. To abide in the Son concerns the sonship of Christ.

Abiding in the Father

Also, we need to be those who are abiding in the Father (v. 24c). How good it is to have a Father! Our Father is all capable. Our Father is always living. Our Father never gets old. He takes care of us in every way and in everything. If a person loses his father, he becomes an orphan. Thank the Lord that God is our Father and that we are not orphans but sons. We are not only abiding in Christ as the organism of the Triune God, in the Lord with His lordship, and in the Son with His sonship, but we are also abiding in the Father with all His care. When we are living in the Triune God, we are living as sons, not orphans. We have a Father. We live in the One who takes care of us.

Our abiding in the Son and in the Father are both mentioned in 1 John 2:24. When we have the Son, we have the Father, because the Son and the Father are one. The Father is in the Son, and the Son is in the Father (John 14:10). When we abide in the Son, we abide in the Father. Our experiences confirm this fact. While we are abiding in the Son, we have the sensation that the Father is with us. We have the Lord, and we have the Father. We have the Son with the Father. When we abide in the Son, we enjoy the fatherhood because the Father is there.

Abiding in God

We also need to be those who are abiding in God (1 John 3:24a). All these different titles—*the Lord, the Son, the Father,* and *God*—bear some significance. In order to understand what it means to abide in God, we need to read 1 John 3:22-24: "Whatever we ask we receive from Him because we keep His commandments and do the things that are pleasing in His sight. And this is His commandment, that we believe in the name of His Son Jesus Christ and love one another, even as He

gave a commandment to us. And he who keeps His commandments abides in Him, and He in him. And in this we know that
He abides in us, by the Spirit whom He gave to us." God is the
One who gave the commandments. These commandments are
that we have to believe in His Son and that we have to love one
another. We need to have the faith in Jesus Christ, the Son
of God, and we need to have the love to love all the brothers.
This is what it means to abide in God. This is a living that
includes the main things of our Christian life. Our Christian
life is a life that believes in Christ and loves the brothers. As
long as we believe in Christ and love all other Christians as our
brothers, we are complete. This means that we are abiding in
God. We abide in God because we are keeping His commandments, which charge us to believe in His Son and to love all the
brothers of His Son. This is to have faith and love.

In 1 John we see that we need to abide in the Lord, in the
Son, in the Father, and in God. This presents a full portrait of
living in the Triune God. To live in the Triune God is to have a
daily life in Christ as the organism of the Triune God, in the
Lord with His headship, with His lordship, in the Son with His
sonship, in the Father with His fatherhood, and in God with
His commandments of believing in His Son and of loving all
His other sons. This is what it means to experience the Divine
Trinity in our daily life.

By the Spirit of God

We abide in God by the Spirit of God (v. 24b). Without the
Spirit of God there is nothing between us and God. The linking, the connection, between us and God, the Father, the Son,
the Lord, and Christ is the Spirit. This "linking Spirit" is in our
spirit. If we are going to enjoy a life of abiding in God, we must
exercise our spirit, turn to our spirit, touch our spirit, and use
our spirit. Then we will touch the linking Spirit. *we exercise our spirit*

According to the Teaching
of the Anointing of the Triune God

the link of God to you.

We abide in the Triune God by the person of the linking
Spirit and according to the teaching of the anointing of the
Triune God (2:27). By studying the context of 1 John 2:27, we

can see that the anointing is of the Triune God. The pronouns *Him* and *His* refer both to the Son and the Father who were previously mentioned (v. 24). They may also refer to the eternal life (v. 25). The anointing is the anointing of the Father, the Son, and the eternal life.

The anointing is the moving and working of the indwelling compound Spirit, the compound ointment. This ointment is similar to paint, which is composed of certain elements. This ointment is divine ointment, divine paint. In this divine paint are the element of the Father, the element of the Son, and the element of the eternal life. This divine ointment, this divine paint, is typified in Exodus 30 by the anointing oil, the compound ointment (vv. 23-25). The move of this ointment is the anointing. We have such an anointing within us, and this anointing teaches us. We have to learn to abide in this wonderful One, who is Christ, the Lord, the Son, the Father, and God. We have to abide in such a wonderful One, not only by the linking Spirit but also according to the teaching of the move of this ointment.

When we are in the meetings of the church or of the ministry, we have a deep and clear sensation that something is moving within us. This is the Spirit as the ointment moving within us. There is a divine paint moving within us. By this moving of the ointment, this anointing, we are made clear concerning what we should be, what we should say, whom we should contact, where we should go, and what we should do. If we are abiding in Christ, the Lord, the Son, the Father, and God, we will live according to the teaching of the anointing in all the affairs of our daily life. Sometimes the inner anointing tells us not to laugh that much, so we have to be one with Him. The anointing teaches us. This is the anointing of the divine paint, which is a composition of the Father and the Son with His eternal life. These elements are marvelous. The sonship, the fatherhood, and the eternal life are compounded into the compound ointment that moves in us, and that moving is the anointing. This anointing teaches us at all times so that we can know His will, His heart's desire, His very nature, and His being. By His teaching, we know what kind of person the inner anointing wants us to be. To live according to the teaching of the anointing of the Triune God is to live in the Divine Trinity.

CHAPTER NINE

LIVING IN THE DIVINE TRINITY

(2)

Scripture Reading: John 14:19-20; 6:57b-58; Gal. 5:25; Phil. 1:20-21a; Gal. 2:20c; Phil. 1:19; Gal. 6:18

In this chapter we want to continue our fellowship concerning our living in the Divine Trinity. When we use the word *living,* we mean *abiding.* Living in the Divine Trinity is abiding in the Divine Trinity. To abide is not merely to remain, to stay, but to dwell, to have our home in a place. Our abiding in the Divine Trinity includes our entire living, our daily walk. Thus, to abide in the Triune God is to dwell in the Triune God, to have our home in the Triune God, to live in the Triune God. The Triune God is embodied in the Son, and the Son as the embodiment of the Triune God with all His members is the organism of the Divine Trinity to produce fruit for the expression of the Triune God. As we abide, live, in the Triune God, we bear fruit for His expression.

LIVING BY THE RESURRECTED CHRIST

Our living in the Divine Trinity is wrapped up with the resurrected Christ. Before Christ's resurrection transpired, no one could live in the Triune God. Our Christ is the resurrected Christ, the pneumatic Christ. John 6 unveils to us how Christ was processed to become the resurrected Christ to indwell us. The outline from the Recovery Version can be a great help to us in seeing this revelation. The outline tells us that verses 32 through 71 show that Christ is the food abiding to eternal life. To become our food, Christ was first incarnated. Verses 32 through 51a show the incarnation of Jesus. Jesus as the food abiding to eternal life was incarnated.

Verses 51b through 55 show that Jesus was slain, because the shedding of blood is indicated. In verse 54 the Lord spoke of eating His flesh and drinking His blood. When blood is separate from flesh, it indicates death. Furthermore, His blood has become drinkable, and His flesh has become eatable. This also indicates His being slain.

Verses 56 through 59 show that Christ was resurrected to indwell. In verse 56 the Lord said, "He who eats My flesh and drinks My blood abides in Me and I in him." This indicates that the Lord had to be resurrected that He might abide in us as our life and life supply. In verse 57 He said, "As the living Father has sent Me and I live because of the Father, so he who eats Me, he also shall live because of Me." *Because of* indicates the factor. We live because we have a living factor that supports us to live. This factor is the resurrected Christ. Christ, the One who was slain and resurrected, can be the very living factor by which we live. We eat Him and live because of Him, the resurrected One. Our living because of Him means that He is the factor of our living.

Verses 60 through 62 show us Christ ascended. Verse 62 says, "Then what if you saw the Son of Man ascending to where He was before?" Verses 63 through 65 show us Christ becoming the life-giving Spirit. The Lord was talking about Himself in the flesh, but in verse 63 He said, "It is the Spirit who gives life; the flesh profits nothing." At this point the Spirit who gives life is brought in. After resurrection and through resurrection the Lord Jesus, who had become flesh, became the Spirit who gives life, as is clearly mentioned in 1 Corinthians 15:45. In the next section of verses in John 6, verses 66 through 71, Christ embodied and realized in the word of life is revealed.

It is wonderful to see such a sequence in John 6. In this chapter we see Christ as the food abiding to eternal life incarnated, slain, resurrected to indwell, ascended, becoming the life-giving Spirit, and embodied and realized in the word of life. After being slain, the very Christ entered into His resurrection to be our eatable food. We are now eating a resurrected One.

John 14:19 and 20 show the very Christ as the resurrected One. These verses say, "Yet a little while and the world beholds Me no longer, but you behold Me; because I live, you also shall live. In that day you will know that I am in My Father, and you in Me, and I in you." For a little while, while He was buried, the world would behold Him no longer, because He was slain. For Him to live is for Him to be resurrected. First Peter 1:3 says that we all were regenerated through the resurrection of Jesus Christ. John 14:19 corresponds with 1 Peter 1:3. When Christ lives, we also live. When Christ became living in His resurrection, we all were resurrected with Him. He, including us, came out of death. He lives, and we also live because of Him.

The Lord went on in verse 20 of John 14 to tell the disciples that in the day of resurrection, they would know that He is in His Father, that they are in Him, and that He is in them. We are now in the One who is in resurrection, and the One who is in resurrection, the pneumatic Christ as the life-giving Spirit, is in us. When the Lord was in the flesh, He was only among the disciples and outside of them, but He was not in them. On the evening of the day of His resurrection He came back to His disciples as the pneumatic Christ and breathed Himself into them. When He breathed into them, He told them to receive the holy breath, the Holy Spirit, the holy pneuma, which was just Himself (20:22). After breathing Himself into them, He remained within them as the pneumatic Christ, the life-giving Spirit.

All these divine secrets have been written down in the Bible, but very few throughout the centuries have seen them. We are greatly blessed to see Christ's incarnation, crucifixion, resurrection, ascension, His becoming a life-giving Spirit, and His embodiment and realization in the word of life as revealed in John 6. Christ as the bread of life became a life-giving Spirit, and this life-giving Spirit has been embodied in the Word. Christ as the bread of life is the Spirit and the Word. The Spirit and the Word are life to us. The Spirit is within, and the Word is without. As we enjoy the Spirit and the Word, we enjoy the real essence of the life-giving bread. The life-giving bread is the Spirit with the Word, and the Spirit with the Word is the very Christ in resurrection, the pneumatic Christ.

We are now living in this Christ, who is the embodiment of the Triune God. When we live in Him, we abide in Him. When we abide in Him, we abide in the embodiment, the organism, of the Divine Trinity. We are not merely remaining in Him or staying in Him; we are living in Him and having our being in Him in the way that we live in a home. To live in a home is to have everything concerning your life in that home. This is what it means to live in the Divine Trinity. We are living in such a One who has gone through incarnation, crucifixion, and is now in resurrection. With Him there is nothing dead. With Him everything is living and organic. As we live in this living, organic One, His living Body is built up to express God and to fulfill God's eternal purpose.

LIVING BY CHRIST AS THE LIFE SUPPLY

We need to be those living by Christ as the life supply (vv. 57b-58). The most important thing in living in a home is eating. In the home nothing is as crucial as food. If we are going to live in the Divine Trinity, to abide in the Divine Trinity as our home, we must enjoy Christ as our food. We need to live by Christ as our life supply. He is our food. He is eatable because He is now in resurrection. Because of His crucifixion, our redemption has been completed. Now Christ is good for us to eat. After accomplishing death and resurrection, He became perfected for us to eat Him. Because He is living in resurrection, He is good for us to eat organically.

After His resurrection the Lord trained His disciples to live by Him as their life supply. In John 21 we see the resurrected Christ moving and living with the believers. In this chapter Peter took the lead to go fishing, and the other disciples followed him because they did not have anything to eat. The resurrected Christ as the disciples' life supply had been breathed into them, but Peter took the lead to go away from this life supply. This life supply was inside of the disciples, not in the sea. They should not have gone to the sea. Instead, they should have remained in their spirit. They became distracted from the life supply in them. Even though they fished through the entire night, they caught nothing. Then what was caught by their fishing? In a sense we can say that they "caught Jesus." They were disappointed to the uttermost that they did not catch one fish. All of a sudden Jesus came. His coming indicated to them that He was their life supply.

The Lord Jesus was training them to realize where the life

supply is. The life supply is not in the world, in the sea, but within us. The very Spirit breathed into our being is the life supply. We do not need to "go fishing." We do not need to go to any other source to get our life supply. The only source of our life supply is in our spirit. This supply is the very pneumatic Christ, who is today the life-giving Spirit indwelling our spirit. John 20 and 21 reveal that the pneumatic Christ came into His disciples to dwell there as the life supply. We should not be distracted from this source to anyone or anything else. Day by day we need to live by the resurrected Christ as the life supply. This is what it means to live, to abide, to have our living, to have our being, in the Divine Trinity.

After this fellowship we may still wonder what it means to live in resurrection. This is very hard to explain. The only thing I can say to explain this is from the negative side. Whenever we are in ourselves, we realize that we are not in resurrection. Whenever we do or say something in a natural way, we know that what we do or say is not in resurrection. As long as we are natural, that is altogether not in resurrection. To be in resurrection is to reject ourselves, our natural man, our natural way, and our old man.

In 1932 a small church was raised up by the Lord in my hometown of Chefoo. Brother Nee heard the good news that a church was raised up in northern China. That was the start of the recovery in northern China, so he was happy. In the spring of 1932 he came to stay with us, and he was my guest. During that time he related an illustration to me that I will never forget. He spoke of the difference between putting a little rock or a living seed into the earth. If we plant the rock in the earth and wait for many years, nothing will come out. If we plant a seed, such as a grain of wheat, something will eventually come out. He asked me why nothing will happen with the buried rock, whereas something will happen with the buried seed. Of course, I responded by saying that this is because there is no life in the rock, whereas there is life in the seed. Then he came to his point. He said, "Brother, we are not a piece of rock. We are a seed. The more we reject ourselves, our flesh, our old man, and the more we become nothing, the more the life within us will rise up."

We are not unbelieving Gentiles, who are like pieces of dead rock. We are regenerated believers. We were regenerated in Christ's resurrection. Now we are living seeds. Within us there is something of resurrection. Within us is the resurrected Christ, the pneumatic Christ as the life-giving Spirit. Therefore, when we reject ourselves, our natural man, our old man, this gives the indwelling, pneumatic Christ the opportunity to grow within us. I received so much help when Brother Nee gave me that simple illustration fifty-five years ago. For fifty-five years I have been enjoying and experiencing the help from that illustration. I am always reminded of what it is to live in the resurrection life. To live in the resurrection life is to deny ourselves, to reject our old man, and to despise the natural way. When we do this, we are immediately in resurrection. This resurrection is a living person.

On another occasion Brother Nee gave a message telling us that the Spirit is the reality and essence of resurrection. Resurrection is the Spirit. This Spirit is not merely the Spirit of God as He was in Genesis 1, brooding upon the surface of the waters. Resurrection is the person of the Spirit of Jesus Christ after Jesus' resurrection. This living person is the reality and the essence of resurrection. To live in resurrection is to live and to walk not by ourselves but by this Spirit. Where is this Spirit? He is right now in our spirit (Rom. 8:16; 1 Cor. 6:17). Thus, whenever we turn to our spirit, we meet the reality of the resurrection, which is a living person, the life-giving Spirit as the pneumatic Christ.

LIVING AND WALKING BY THE SPIRIT

In order to live in the Divine Trinity, we need to live and walk by the Spirit. Galatians 5:25 says, "If we live by the Spirit, let us also walk by the Spirit." To live by the Spirit is somewhat general, but to walk by the Spirit is particular. To live by the Spirit is to have our life dependent upon and regulated by the Spirit. To walk by the Spirit in verse 25 means to walk orderly or to march in military rank. The Spirit by whom we live and walk is the pneumatic Christ. The pneumatic Christ is resurrection itself. When we live by the Spirit and walk by the Spirit, we live and walk by and in resurrection.

The Lord Jesus told us that He is the resurrection and the

life (John 11:25). Life and resurrection are not things but a person. Resurrection is a living person who is life that has gone through death. Resurrection is the expression of life that has passed through death and has been tested, checked out, by death. Before being checked out by death, life was purely life, not resurrection. But after being checked out by death and passing through death successfully, life has become resurrection. Both life and resurrection are the same wonderful, excellent person. This person is the pneumatic Christ as the life-giving Spirit. This Spirit is the resurrection, in which we Christians should live all the time.

To live in this resurrection is to forget about ourselves, to renounce ourselves, to deny ourselves. When we go out to preach the gospel or to do anything in service to the Lord, we should act not in ourselves but in Christ, in resurrection, in the pneumatic Christ, in the living Spirit, who gives life to us all the time as our life supply. Every item of the God-ordained way should be carried out in resurrection. Preaching the gospel, baptizing people, having home meetings, having group meetings, and prophesying in the larger meetings of the church should be done by our renouncing, rejecting, and denying ourselves. This means that everything should be done in resurrection.

LIVING CHRIST FOR HIS MAGNIFICATION

To live in the Divine Trinity is to live Christ for His magnification (Phil. 1:20-21a). No one in himself can live Christ for His magnification. We live Christ for His magnification only through the bountiful supply of the Spirit of Jesus Christ (v. 19). When we live by the Spirit and walk by the Spirit, spontaneously we live Christ to magnify Him. The factor, the element, and the sphere of our living should be the life-giving Spirit, the Spirit of Jesus Christ as the bountiful supply. The term *the Spirit of Jesus Christ* means that the Spirit is Jesus Christ. He is the rich Spirit as our life supply, and He is in our spirit. This is why we need to stress the matter of our spirit. We cannot overstress this matter. We have to stress this matter again and again. We need to turn to our spirit, exercise our spirit, and stir up our spirit because in our spirit is the very resurrection, who is the living One, the pneumatic Christ, the life-giving Spirit.

The secret of experiencing this One is to deny ourselves. As long as we deny ourselves, we are in resurrection, but it is different with the unbelieving Gentiles because they do not have this treasure of resurrection in their spirit. Their spirit is dead and has not been regenerated, but our spirit is different. Our spirit has been regenerated. Christ as the resurrected One is within our regenerated spirit as the very resurrection. Thus, we can live in the Divine Trinity because the very embodiment of this Divine Trinity is in our spirit as the resurrection. We can live in and by the resurrected Christ as the resurrection itself. Whenever we deny ourselves, renounce our soul, we enter into the full realization and experience of this resurrection.

This is altogether in faith, not in our feelings. We have to exercise our faith to believe this. Faith is the substantiating of the fact. In this universe and especially within us, there is a fact, a reality, which we cannot see. However, we can substantiate this fact. The verb *substantiate* comes from the noun *substance*. All the spiritual things, especially Christ being resurrection within us, must be substantiated by our faith. Faith comes out of the hearing of the word (Rom. 10:17). As we hear the word, the good things concerning Christ, we see a vision, and this seeing produces an appreciation, a faith, within us. Our faith is our appreciation of the Lord Jesus Christ. When we hear Him and see Him, spontaneously there is an appreciation within us. This appreciation is the believing, the faith, and this faith is the faith of the Son of God (Gal. 2:20c). The faith of the Son of God is actually the faith as the Son of God. This faith is Jesus Christ Himself.

BY THE GRACE OF THE LORD JESUS CHRIST
IN THE BELIEVERS' SPIRIT

Eventually, what we see, what we believe, what we appreciate, and what we get is the grace. Grace is the resurrected Christ as our enjoyment. The closing verse of the book of Galatians says, "The grace of our Lord Jesus Christ be with your spirit, brothers. Amen" (6:18). By this grace we experience the resurrected Christ, who is the embodiment of the Divine Trinity. Christ, the pneumatic One, is our resurrection producing the faith for our enjoyment of Him as grace. We live in the Divine Trinity by the grace of the Lord Jesus in our spirit.

QUESTIONS AND ANSWERS

Question: We are talking about living in resurrection by denying ourselves. When we live in this way, does this cause us to grow and be transformed, or do we need to grow and be transformed before we can live in this way?

Answer: *Hymns,* #481 is an excellent hymn on being identified with the Lord in His death and resurrection. The first two lines of stanza 2 say,

'Tis not hard to die with Christ
When His risen life we know.

This hymn was written by A. B. Simpson. All those who know the inner life love this hymn. The question that was asked is actually a question concerning whether we have death first and then resurrection, or resurrection first and then death. By the illustration of the seed being buried in the earth, we can see the sequence. The seed has life in it; life is resurrection. But without being buried in the earth, the seed will not be glorified. Being buried in the earth is equivalent to denying, rejecting, and renouncing ourselves. The multiplication of life, the glorification of life, as resurrection is by this burial, this renouncing.

The Lord came with life, but He passed through death. Then He entered into resurrection for His multiplication, His increase, His glorification. Today we can receive Him as our life, making us a seed. In order for us as the seed to express the divine life for its multiplication, increase, glorification, we need to go through the death that He has gone through. Going through His death is the conformity to His death.

We can see in Philippians 3 that Paul had Christ as life and that he lived by that life, yet he aspired to know more. He wanted to know Christ and the power of His resurrection, being conformed to His death. We have Christ as life already, yet we need to know Him more. The increased knowing of Christ and of the power of resurrection will strengthen us to pass through His death. By knowing Him more, we can be conformed unto His death. This is clearly portrayed in the book of Philippians, which is a book on the experience of Christ. The conformity to His death is the renouncing of ourselves, the denying of ourselves, the rejecting of ourselves. Rejecting, renouncing, and denying mean the same thing. When we deny ourselves, we live in resurrection.

Question: Could you share something concerning Romans 8:13, which says, "If by the Spirit you put to death the practices of the body, you will live"?

Answer: Romans 8:13 also shows us something concerning the conformity to the death of Christ. We have the Holy Spirit within us, yet there are still many negative things in our mortal body. Life can enter into our mortal body by the indwelling Spirit (v. 11). The indwelling Spirit is the reality of resurrection. This reality of resurrection, as the very inner life within us, can reach our mortal body. In order for this to happen, we have to cooperate with Him by putting every action, every deed, of our body to death. This is our cooperation with the indwelling Spirit so that we can be conformed to the death of Christ and live in and by the resurrected Christ.

CHAPTER TEN

LIVING WITH THE DIVINE TRINITY

(1)

Scripture Reading: John 15:5, 7-8, 16; 14:17; 1 John 3:24a; John 14:23, 21-22; Gal. 2:20b; Rom. 8:9-11, 2, 6

We have seen that to live in the Divine Trinity is to dwell in Him as our home. To live in Him is to abide in Him, to remain in Him. The Lord said, "Abide in Me and I in you" (John 15:4). Thus, abiding in Him is a condition of His abiding in us. Whether or not He would abide in us depends upon our abiding in Him. To live in Christ, to abide in Christ, is the first part of our enjoyment of the Triune God. In this chapter we come to the second part of our enjoyment. This part of our enjoyment is conveyed by the Lord's word concerning His abiding in us. His abiding in us brings His presence to us, so we live with Him. To live in Him puts us into the position of the enjoyment of the Lord. To live with Him is the enjoyment itself. To live with the Divine Trinity is to enjoy the Divine Trinity. To live with a person is to enjoy that person. Thus, to live with the Triune God is our enjoyment of the Triune God.

According to my rough estimation, one-fourth of the New Testament is for our living in the Triune God, but three-fourths of the New Testament is for our living with the Triune God. To live with the Triune God covers nearly the entire New Testament revelation. The final revelation of the entire Bible, in Revelation 22, is the eternal part of our living with the Triune God. Revelation 22 reveals the throne of God and of the Lamb, out of which proceeds the river of water of life (v. 1). On the two sides of this river grows the tree of life, yielding its fruit each month to be the food of God's redeemed for eternity (v. 2). God's redeemed will be His slaves and His priests (v. 3). While they are serving God, they will see God's face, and the Triune God's name will be on their foreheads (v. 4). This indicates that they are one with the Triune God. Bearing the name of the Triune God not only indicates that we belong to Him but also that we are one with Him.

In eternity we all will have the name of the Triune God on our foreheads. We will drink the river of water of life, eat the tree of life, and enjoy God as our light of life. According to Revelation 22:5, we will not need the light of a lamp made by man or the light of the sun created by God. We will only need and only have God Himself as our illumination. We will enjoy Him as our light, and we will also enjoy reigning in and with Him as kings forever and ever. This is the last view, the last vision, of the entire Bible. This is the eternal part of our enjoying the Triune God. This revelation is under the section of living with the Triune God. Our living with the Triune God today will bring us into that enjoyment in eternity.

In eternity the fallen angels and the fallen human beings will live with Satan. Because they will be with Satan, they will partake of whatever Satan will suffer. They will suffer Satan's eternal judgment, the torment of the lake of fire. In the same principle, we will be with our Triune God, so we will enjoy whatever He is. To live with the Triune God is to enjoy Him. We need to see this last vision revealed in the entire Bible. We need to have a bird's-eye view of the entire revelation of the New Testament. This bird's-eye view is that one-fourth of the New Testament is concerning our living in the Triune God, whereas three-fourths is concerning our living with the Triune God.

HAVING CHRIST ABIDING IN US

To live in the Divine Trinity is to abide in Christ, and to live with the Divine Trinity is to have Christ abide in us (John 15:5). When we abide in Christ, Christ abides in us, and His abiding is His presence with us. When He abides in us, we have His presence. We have Him with us for our enjoyment.

Having the Words of Christ Abiding in Us for the Bearing of Remaining Fruit

To have Christ abiding in us is to have the words of Christ

abiding in us for the bearing of remaining fruit (vv. 7-8, 16). In
John 15:7 the Lord said, "If you abide in Me and My words abide
in you, ask whatever you will, and it shall be done for you." This
kind of asking is related to fruit-bearing (v. 8) and surely will
be fulfilled. If we are to be those who go forth to preach the gospel, we must be those who love the word of Christ. We must be
those who have the living word, the word of life, abiding in us.
If we are not such persons, our preaching of the gospel will not
last long. The living word of Christ stirs us up to go forth and
bear fruit. The word of Christ abiding in us brings us the enjoyment of all that the Triune God is. This encourages us, stirs us
up, burdens us, and charges us to go forth to preach the gospel
to people. The bubbling of His words infuse the reality into people.

     If we do not have the word of Christ abiding in us, we may
go out to reach people, but what we do will be in a poor way. The
content and the issue of what we do will be vain, empty. If we are
going to do a rich work, a work full of the riches of the Triune
God, we must have the word of Christ abiding in us. Then when
we talk to people, we will not talk to them with our own opin-
ion, our own thought, our own word, our own expression, or our
own utterance. We will talk to people with the word of Christ.
This is why Paul charges us in Colossians 3:16 to let the word
of Christ dwell, abide, in us richly. We need to have a storage of
the word of Christ in us. Then what we speak will be the word
of Christ, which expresses the very riches of Christ. To have the
word of Christ abide in us is a rich enjoyment of the Triune
God.   His Word

Having the Spirit of Reality Abiding in Us

     To have Christ abiding in us is to have the Spirit of real-
ity abiding in us (John 14:17). John 14—16 is a long message
given by the Lord just before He was betrayed. In chapter 15 the
Lord mentioned His words abiding in us, and in chapter 14 He
spoke of the Spirit of reality abiding in us. Actually, the words
of Christ and the Spirit of reality are one. In John 6:63 the Lord
told us that the words which He has spoken are spirit. God's
word and God the Spirit are both God's breath. When this breath
gets into us and remains in us, this breath is the Spirit. When
this breath comes out of us through our speaking, it becomes

the word. When we breathe in the word of the Bible, the word becomes the Spirit in us. We contact our Triune God through the Spirit and in the word. We enjoy Him through the Spirit in our spirit and in the word. As long as we have His words abiding in us, this issues in the Spirit abiding in us. The more His words abide in us, the more the Spirit abides in us. These are two aspects of the breath of our Triune God.

The reality of the word is Spirit. We need to touch it with our spirit.

Having God Abiding in Us

First John 3:24a speaks of God abiding in us. The word, the Spirit, and God are one. Both the word and the Spirit are the reality of the Triune God. The word is the Spirit, and the Spirit is God. These three are one for our enjoyment.

Having the Son and the Father Coming to Us and Making an Abode with Us

To have Christ abiding in us is to have the Son and the Father coming to us and making an abode with us (John 14:23). When we have the words of Christ, the Spirit of reality, and the very God abiding in us, we surely have the Son and the Father abiding in us. We have both the Son and the Father coming to us and making an abode with us. This abode is a mutual abode. He becomes our abode, and we become His abode.

The New Jerusalem is a mutual abode. The Triune God in eternity will abide in His chosen people, and His chosen people will abide in Him. His chosen people will be His abode, and He Himself will be their abode. This is why the New Jerusalem, the holy city, is, on the one hand, a temple and, on the other hand, a tabernacle. It is a tabernacle for God's dwelling and a temple for our dwelling in which we live to serve God. The New Jerusalem will be a tabernacle to God and a temple to us.

He loves us and He wants us to love Him

love Him. It is needed before He visit us, makes home in us.

The Son and the Father come to us and make an abode with us because of our loving the Son. The Son and the Father's making an abode with us depends upon whether or not we love the Lord Jesus. When we tell the Lord Jesus that we love Him, we will sense His coming to us and making His abode with us. If we neglect our love toward Him, we will lose His manifestation, His appearing. When Peter and the other disciples went fishing, as recorded in John 21, they thought that they were absent from the Lord. They did not know that the Lord was still with them. He was with them, but at the time of their fishing they did not have His manifestation, His appearing. If we say, "Lord Jesus, I love You," we will not only have Him with us but also have Him appearing to us, manifesting Himself to us. His coming to us and making an abode with us is His appearing, His manifestation.

In John 14:23 the Lord said, "If anyone loves Me,…My Father will love him." When we love the Son, the Father will love us. Then the Son will follow His Father to love us (v. 21). The Father and the Son both will love us because we love the Son. This issues in our enjoyment of the Son's manifestation (vv. 21-22). Our enjoyment of the Son's manifestation depends upon our loving Him. This is altogether not a doctrine but an experience. The Divine Trinity is not for doctrine but altogether for our experience. When we love the Son, both the Father and the Son love us, and at the same time the Son manifests Himself to us. We enjoy His appearing. In other words, we enjoy His presence.

HAVING THE RESURRECTED CHRIST LIVING IN US

To live with the Divine Trinity is to have the resurrected Christ living in us (Gal. 2:20b). The apostle Paul declares two wonderful things. In Galatians 2:20 he declares that he was crucified with Christ and that it was no longer he who lived, but Christ lived in him. In Philippians 1:21 he declares that to him to live was Christ. On the one hand, he lived Christ, and on the other hand, Christ lived in him. The Christ who lived in him was the resurrected Christ, the Christ in resurrection.

HAVING THE SPIRIT OF GOD HOUSING IN US

To live with the Divine Trinity is also to have the Spirit of God housing in us (Rom. 8:9-11). Romans 8:9 speaks of the Spirit of God dwelling in us. The word for *dwells* in th means "to house," "to reside." The indwelling Spi in us. This means that we have the Spirit of Chr the pneumatic Christ in us (v. 10), and the resur us (v. 11). Such a housing of the Spirit, with Christ and the resurrecting God, gives life eve bodies (v. 11).

dispensing Himself into us.

Romans 8:9-11 reveals the living we have with the Triune God. The Triune God is a housing factor to impart life into our entire tripartite being—into our spirit, our mind, and our body. When the Spirit of God houses in us, we have the Spirit as the firstfruits (v. 23). The firstfruits of the Spirit means that the firstfruits are the Spirit. When we live with the Divine Trinity, we have the Spirit as the firstfruits, which means that we have the Spirit as our enjoyment.

BY THE LAW OF THE SPIRIT OF LIFE

Romans 8:2

We live with the Divine Trinity by the law of the Spirit of life (v. 2). The law of the Spirit of life referred to by Paul in Romans 8 is not the law in letters but a natural principle. There are natural principles that operate in the universe. These principles are laws, such as the law of gravity. If we drop something, it will fall to the ground because of the gravitational factor. Gravity is a spontaneous power and a natural principle. It is amazing that nearly two thousand years ago the apostle Paul saw the law of the Spirit of life. He was not a scientist, yet he understood the laws in nature and in the divine realm. The law of the Spirit of life is a natural power. It is a natural force just like the law of gravity. A plane is able to overcome the law of gravity by a higher law, which we may call the law of aerodynamics. We have a higher law within us, and this law is the law of the Spirit of life.

This law is a triune person. When the Father, the Son, and the Spirit move in us, They are the law. The law of the Spirit of life within us is the moving Triune God. When the Triune God is moving within us, there is a spontaneous force, a spontaneous power, to carry out something. However, there are some obstacles within us that prevent Him from going further. Thus, He is stopped. This is why this law, the moving Triune God, needs the cross to cross out all the obstacles. The killing of the cross brings in another law to annul all the obstacles. Romans 8:13 reveals that if we cooperate with the indwelling Spirit to put all the deeds and activities of our body to death, we will have the law of the Spirit of life working within us without any obstacles. Then we will live.

natural man doesn't have one.

This law of the Spirit of life is the spontaneous working of the Divine Trinity—the Spirit of God, the Spirit of Christ, and Christ (vv. 9-10). This law frees us from the law of sin and of death (v. 2b). The law of the Spirit of life is God, and the law of sin and of death is the devil. The devil, Satan, is another law. We have two laws within us. In our first birth, our natural birth, Satan was brought into our being as the law of sin and of death. In our second birth, our regeneration, the Triune God was brought into us as the law of the Spirit of life. The law of the Spirit of life frees us from the law of sin and of death.

Furthermore, this law of the Spirit of life imparts life into our spirit, mind, and body (vv. 10, 6, 11). This issues in peace (v. 6). This is not the outward peace in our circumstances but the peace within us, in our inner being. If we Christians do not have the inner peace, this is an indicator that we are wrong. This means that the law of the Spirit of life has no way to work in us. As long as we have peace in the depths of our inner being, that is a positive indicator that the law of the Spirit of life, the Triune God—the Father, the Son, and the Spirit—is working in us. We live with the Divine Trinity by the law of the Spirit of life. This is our enjoyment of the Triune God.

when we don't have peace, it means that
He is not with us.

CHAPTER ELEVEN

LIVING WITH THE DIVINE TRINITY

(2)

Scripture Reading: 1 Cor. 1:24, 30; 2:10; 6:19, 17; 12:13; 2 Cor.
1:21-22; 2:14-15; 10:1; 11:10; Eph. 3:16-19; Gal. 4:19; 1:15-16a;
3:27; 2:20; 3:29; Eph. 1:13b-14; 1 Pet. 1:4

In this chapter we want to continue our fellowship concerning living with the Divine Trinity. To live with the Divine Trinity is the enjoyment and the experience of the Divine Trinity.

CHRIST BECOMING POWER AND WISDOM TO US FROM GOD: BOTH RIGHTEOUSNESS AND SANCTIFICATION AND REDEMPTION

To live with the Divine Trinity is to have Christ become power and wisdom to us from God: both righteousness and sanctification and redemption (1 Cor. 1:24, 30). Christ is both power and wisdom from God to us. To us indicates a transmission. This is similar to the electricity installed into a building. In order to experience and apply the electricity, the switch must be turned on. Then there is the transmission of the electricity. Christ is both power and wisdom transmitted from God to us like the transmission of electricity. This transmission is not once for all. We use the electricity in a building day after day. Day after day we switch on the electricity to enjoy the transmission of electricity. In the same way, we need to enjoy the continual transmission of Christ as power and wisdom from God to us.

According to 1 Corinthians 1:30, Christ as our wisdom is all-inclusive. Christ became wisdom to us from God as righteousness, sanctification, and redemption. Righteousness is for our

The Spirit won't come into a sinful vessel. He died for us that we can be cleansed.

past. By Christ as our righteousness, we have been justified by God that we might be reborn in our spirit to receive the divine life (Rom. 5:18). Sanctification is for our present. By Christ as our sanctification, we are being sanctified in our soul, that is, transformed in our mind, emotion, and will with His divine life (6:19, 22). Redemption is for our future. Christ as our redemption is for the redemption of our body (8:23), by which we will be transfigured in our body with His divine life to have His glorious likeness (Phil. 3:21). Righteousness, sanctification, and redemption are included in Christ as our wisdom. This wisdom is to us from God as a continual transmission for our experience and enjoyment.

It is of God that we are in Christ (1 Cor. 1:30a). We were put into Christ by God so that He could be both power and wisdom to us in a continuous way. This has been revealed to us through the Spirit (2:10). The unveiling Spirit reveals the depths of God to us through God's holy Word for our deep experience and deep enjoyment. First Corinthians 6:19 says that our body is a temple of the Holy Spirit, who is in us and whom we have from God. The Spirit is the means, the element, and the sphere for our experience of the wonderful Christ. Our body is a temple for the unveiling Spirit. We have to treasure the fact that our body is a holy temple, sanctified for the consummated Spirit of the Triune God. He is lodged in our being, taking our being as His dwelling place.

Because of the indwelling Spirit in our spirit, we are joined to the Lord as one spirit (v. 17). It is a wonder that our human spirit is mingled, or joined, with the divine Spirit into one! The two spirits have been merged into one spirit. The relationship between us and God has arrived at such a marvelous state that we and God are one in the spirit. As proper, normal Christians, we must learn to remain in our spirit. We should always come back to our spirit, exercise our spirit, and use our spirit. To experience and enjoy God, Christ, and the Spirit, we need to be in our spirit all the time. We should always stay here and dwell here. We need to be those enjoying the Triune God in our spirit.

First Corinthians 12:13 says that we were all given to drink one Spirit. First, the Spirit dwells in us. Then He becomes our drink. The Spirit of God is our drink, and the Word of God is our food. Day by day we should eat the Word of God and drink the Spirit of God as our living water.

All the items of Christ revealed in the book of 1 Corinthians can be experienced and enjoyed by us only in and through the all-inclusive Spirit. God has made Christ our power and wisdom in and through the Spirit.

GOD HAVING GIVEN US
THE PLEDGE OF THE SPIRIT IN OUR HEARTS

Second Corinthians 1:22 says that God has given us the pledge of the Spirit in our hearts. According to 2 Corinthians 1:21-22, God has anointed us and firmly attaches us unto Christ. He has also sealed us. Based upon this, God manifests the fragrance of Christ through us for others' salvation (2:14-15). The saving power is the fragrance of Christ going out from us. This fragrance is actually the living Spirit. The fragrance that goes out from us may be compared to the steam that goes out from a vaporizer. A vaporizer converts water into steam so that others can breathe it in. When they breathe the air, they receive the water as well. This is similar to the fragrance that goes out from our Christian being to save others. When they breathe in this fragrance, they receive Christ. When we go out to visit people for the preaching of the gospel, they should be able to breathe in the fragrance of Christ.

Christ has been ministered to us for us to become letters written with the Spirit as ink (3:3). We are living letters. A letter conveys a revelation of a certain thing or a certain person. As the living letters of Christ, we convey the beautiful and wonderful person of Christ. We are His living letters conveying Him to people. We have been inscribed, or written on, with the element of the living Spirit of God as the ink.

In chapters 2 through 4 of 2 Corinthians Paul uses five very significant and expressive metaphors as illustrations of what the believers should be. The first metaphor is that we are captives in a triumphant procession for the celebration of Christ's victory (2:14a). We were captives under Satan's hand, but Christ has rescued us and made us His captives. We are captives in His triumphant procession to celebrate His all-inclusive victory.

Then we are incense-bearers to scatter the fragrance of Christ (vv. 14b-16). Chapter 3 shows that we are letters written with the Spirit of God to convey Christ to others (vv. 1-3) and mirrors beholding and reflecting the glory of Christ in order to be transformed into His glorious image (v. 18). On the one hand, we are the letters conveying Christ. On the other hand, we are mirrors reflecting Christ in our transformation by the Lord Spirit. Finally, we are the earthen vessels that contain the Triune God in Christ as the excellent treasure (4:7). The above five metaphors are used to describe, to illustrate, or to portray the real experience and enjoyment that we have in the processed Triune God embodied in Christ and consummated as the Spirit. Today this wonderful Spirit is indwelling our spirit. Whenever we are in our spirit, we are with this wonderful Triune God. We are with the consummated Spirit, with the embodied Christ, and with the processed Triune God. We are experiencing Him and enjoying Him as captives, as incense-bearers, as letters, as mirrors, and as vessels.

Furthermore, we are being transformed into the image of Christ by the Lord Spirit (3:17-18). As we experience the Triune God, we are being transformed into the image of Christ as the embodiment of the Triune God by the consummated Spirit as the Lord. When I was a young Christian, I heard messages on God's chastening and disciplining, but I did not hear anything concerning transformation. Eventually, the Lord brought me out of that old field into a new field. My understanding of the Bible changed. We need a new view to see the processed Triune God embodied in Christ and consummated as the Spirit. Everything that we have been talking about in these chapters is covered by the phrase *the processed Triune God embodied in Christ and consummated as the Spirit.*

Second Corinthians 5 goes on to show us that God has wrought us for our transfiguration with the Spirit as the pledge (vv. 2-5). Verse 17 says that we are a new creation in Christ. Many Christians know this verse, but they do not know the real significance of this term *the new creation.* We have to realize that we were not only regenerated but also re-created. We were regenerated to be a new man and re-created to be a new creation. We are in another creation. We do not belong to the old creation, and we are not in the old creation. Now we are in the new creation as a new man.

Eventually, 2 Corinthians reveals that we need to express the virtues of Christ as meekness, forbearance, and truthfulness (10:1; 11:10). Our Christian virtues are a product of the divine virtues of God. The five metaphors that we have seen in 2 Corinthians 2—4 are great items, whereas the virtues of Christ mentioned in chapters 10 and 11 may be considered as small items. This shows that the all-inclusive Christ covers not only big items but also the small, fine items of the Christian virtues. In the *Life-study of Philippians* we gave seven messages on the subject of forbearance (see Messages 56 through 62 of the *Life-study of Philippians*). In those messages I contrasted forbearance with anxiety. If we would have forbearance, we must be released from anxiety. It is difficult to express the real meaning of the Greek word for *forbearance*. This word means "reasonableness, considerateness, and consideration in dealing with others without strictness of legal right." This implies that we can fit in any kind of situation to meet the need of any kind of person. It means that we are humble, that we can give in to others, and that we are able to fit any situation and any circumstance with anybody. A forbearing person can fit in with both the older generation and the younger generation.

Forbearance seemingly is a small virtue, but actually, it is great. If we are forbearing persons, we are great persons. If I easily lose my temper when someone makes a mistake, am I a great person? When we lose our temper in this way, we are small persons. A great person embraces all kinds of people. A forbearing person, a great person, can embrace even the ones who oppose him. The Lord Jesus charged us in Matthew 5:44 to love our enemies and pray for those who persecute us. This is the expression of forbearance.

I have seen some saints who have been offended and would never forget that offense. Some wives never forget how their husbands have offended them. In the biblical sense, to forgive is to forget. Without forgetting, forgiving means nothing. If we do not forget others' offenses, this means that we have not forgiven them. Forgiving is forgetting. When God forgives us, He washes away the stain of our sin (Psa. 51:7; 1 John 1:7).

Furthermore, He remembers our sins no more (Heb. 8:12). We need to be one with our God to forgive people to such an extent.

A new church in a new locality is always sweet, and the church life there is in the "honeymoon stage." However, after the church has been there for ten years, the offenses accumulate. This mountain of offenses can kill the entire church life. Among all the local churches on the earth, it is hard to find one that has been existing for over five years without the accumulation of offenses. These offenses are a big stumbling block. We have to stop to move this stumbling block, this mountain, out of the way. Then we can drive on, and the church life can go on. Why is it that a couple can be married for many years, yet they can become separated and then divorced? This is because of the accumulated offenses. The husband offends the wife, and the wife offends the husband again and again with no mutual forgiveness. This accumulation of offenses leads to separation and then divorce. There is divorce because there is no forbearance. To be proper Christians, we need forbearance. Forbearance implies forgiveness, lowliness, giving in, and fitting in with others under any kind of situation. Paul told us that he had the meekness and forbearance of Christ because he had been attached to Christ. Paul realized that he was one with Christ. Because of this Paul also realized that he had the virtues of Christ's human life. Paul not only enjoyed Christ's divinity in great things but also enjoyed His humanity in the detailed items of Christ's human virtues based upon the divine attributes.

HAVING CHRIST MAKE HIS HOME IN OUR HEARTS

Ephesians 3:16-17a speaks of Christ making His home in our hearts through faith by the Father strengthening us into our inner man through His Spirit with power according to the riches of His glory. Since we love Christ, we need to allow Him to make His home in our hearts through faith. The very presence of Christ within us is substantiated by our faith. In order for Christ to make His home in our hearts, the Father has to strengthen us into our inner man. To understand what it means to be strengthened into our inner man, we need to consider our experience. The more we are not in our spirit, the weaker we are. When we are weak, we are surely absent from our spirit. When

God the Father comes to strengthen us, that strengthening will bring us back to our spirit, which is our very inner man. When we are weak, we are remaining in our outer man, in our flesh, in our self, in our natural man, and in our soul. But when we are strong in the Lord, we are remaining in our spirit, in our inner man.

Because we are not in our inner man much of the time, there was the need of some apostle to pray for us. Paul prayed to the Father, asking the Father to strengthen all the saints, who are weak in their outer man, into their inner man. The Father does not do this strengthening directly. He strengthens the weaker saints through the Spirit with power, and He does this strengthening according to the riches of His glory. This prepares the way, opens the way, paves the way, so that the Son can have a highway to make His home in our entire heart. In our heart there are four rooms—the room of the mind, the room of the will, the room of the emotion, and the room of the conscience. Christ wants to make His home in all these different rooms.

Christ making His home in our hearts results in our having been rooted and grounded in love. To be rooted is for growth, and to be grounded is for building. This rooting and grounding is in love. Christ makes His home in our hearts through faith, and we are rooted and grounded in love. *Through faith* refers to our substantiating; *in love* refers to embracing with a loving heart. To realize that Christ is making His home in our heart, we need faith to substantiate it. To have ourselves rooted for growth and grounded for building, there is the need of love. We need to love the Lord and also love the rooting and the grounding. We need to be those who love the Lord, who love His rooting, and who love His grounding that we may grow and be built up.

When we have been rooted and grounded in our love toward the Lord, we will be strong. We will have the strength, the power, the capability, to apprehend with all the saints the breadth, length, height, and depth of Christ and to know the knowledge-surpassing love of Christ. The breadth and length are horizontal, whereas the height and depth are vertical. These are the dimensions of Christ, which we have to experience. These dimensions make a cube, which is solid, strong, stable, unbreakable, and immovable. We need to apprehend with all the saints the dimensions of this great, universal cube—Christ. We also are made strong to know the knowledge-surpassing love of Christ. This love surpasses knowledge, yet we can know it.

Eventually, this results in our being filled unto all the fullness of God (vv. 17b-19). *Unto* means "resulting in," or "issuing in." Such an experience of Christ making His home in our hearts eventually results in our being filled to such an extent that we become the fullness of the Godhead. This fullness is the very expression of all the riches of the Triune Godhead. The living church, the actual church, the active church, the real church, is the expression of the Triune God.

Today can we see such a church in the universe? We must admit that there is not such a church today. The Triune God will not tolerate this situation. He is doing something to change this situation. This is why we need to pray for one another so that we would be strengthened into our inner man with power through the Father's Spirit according to the riches of His glory that the Lord Jesus may have a way to make His home in our hearts. Then we will love the rooting and the grounding, and we will have the strength to apprehend the universal dimensions of Christ with all the saints. We cannot apprehend by ourselves in an individualistic way. We need all the saints to apprehend the dimensions of the Lord Jesus—the breadth, the length, the height, and the depth. We need to experience Christ as an unbreakable, stable cube. Eventually, we will know the knowledge-surpassing love of Christ, and we all will be filled unto the very fullness of the Triune God as the church according to His heart's desire. We need to pray this prayer recorded in Ephesians 3.

HAVING CHRIST FORMED IN US

To live with the Divine Trinity is to have Christ formed in us (Gal. 4:19). After Christ makes His home in our hearts, He will be formed in us. He will spread Himself from our spirit into every room of our entire inner being. Galatians speaks of God revealing His Son in us (1:15-16a). This is the first step. Then we have been baptized into Christ and have put on Christ (3:27). We have been put into Christ, taking Christ as our clothing, and now Christ takes us as His dwelling by living in us (2:20). Then Christ matures in us. For Christ to mature in us is for Him to be formed in us. He matures in us for us to be heirs (3:29) for the full enjoyment of the Triune God as our inheritance (Eph. 1:14; 1 Pet. 1:4). The Holy Spirit is the pledge of this inheritance (Eph. 1:13b-14a). Thus, the entire Divine Trinity is involved in Christ's being formed in us.

Care for His operation; [conscious of Amen to His operation; and work out His operation.

CHAPTER TWELVE

LIVING WITH THE DIVINE TRINITY

(3)

Abide: not just we abide in Him and He is also doing sth in us (operating)

Scripture Reading: Phil. 2:13; 1:19-21a; 2:15-16a; 3:10-14; 4:8, 12-13

In this chapter we want to see the revelation concerning our living with the Divine Trinity in the book of Philippians.

GOD OPERATING IN US

Philippians 2:13 says, "It is God who operates in you both the willing and the working for His good pleasure." Everything that is covered in the book of Philippians is under God's operating move. God has a move on this earth, and He moves by His operating.

In order to see God's operating in us, it would be helpful for us to have a brief review of the book of Philippians. Philippians is a book concerning our experience of Christ. Chapter 1 shows us that we need to live and magnify Christ for Him to be our living and expression. Chapter 2 shows that we need to take Christ as our pattern and hold Him forth. In chapter 3 we see that we need to pursue and gain Christ as our goal. Chapter 4 shows us that we need to have Christ as our secret of sufficiency. In verse 12 of chapter 4 Paul declares that he has learned the secret. He uses a metaphor concerning a person being initiated into a secret society with instruction in its rudimentary principles. Actually, this "secret society" in chapter 4 is the Body of Christ. In conclusion, we can say that in chapter 1 of Philippians Christ is our living and expression; in chapter 2 He is our pattern; in chapter 3 He is our goal; and in chapter 4 He is our secret. All four chapters reveal a certain aspect of Christ for us to experience.

Chapter 2 gives us the overall thought, the all-embracing thought, the all-inclusive thought, of the book of Philippians. This thought is that the moving God is operating in us. Whatever Christ is to us is for the operating of God. We should care for God's operating in us. Our God is living, moving, and operating in you and me continuously. God's operating in us can be compared to our blood circulation or to the circulation of electricity. If the flow of blood within us stops, our life will stop. The circulation of blood is life operating in us. The flow of electricity is the operating of the electricity. If the flow of electricity stops in a building, there will be no light there.

Many Christians do not think about God's move in this way. Some in the Pentecostal movement like to shout, cry out, and even jump. They like a big, outward display, but God's inward operating in us does not necessarily have such an outward display. The current of electricity in a building is a very good illustration of God's operating. When we enter into the building, it may seem that nothing is working there because everything is quiet. However, there is an operating going on, and this quiet operating is vigorous. The operating of the electricity in the building enables all the appliances, machines, and devices in the building to move and function. If this electricity is switched off, everything in the building is shut down. The more I have experienced God throughout the years, the more I realize that God's move within us is a very quiet, fine operation. He operates in us quietly and finely.

Although we are Christians, it may seem that we have nothing within us. We may wonder at times what the difference is between us and the unbelievers. The truth concerning regeneration and transformation is very high and great. Even though we have been regenerated and are being transformed, we may feel like common persons. Actually, however, God is operating in us. Although a big building is under the operation of electricity, this operation is quiet and calm. We need to see that God's operating in us is a miraculous normality. It is altogether normal yet altogether miraculous.

D. L. Moody said that the greatest miracle in the universe is regeneration. I agree with this. No miracle is greater than regeneration. Regeneration means that we have the divine life in addition to our human life. We have the divine life, but we may not feel that we can see much of the manifestation of this life within us. We may feel that others who are not regenerated are actually better than we are. Even though we are regenerated, we may lose our temper again and again. However, our being better or worse than others is an outward matter. If we are regenerated, we have the inner realization that something is within us. This "something" is the living and moving God who is now operating in us. Whether a person is outwardly bad or good may be according to his natural birth. What matters is not whether we are good or bad according to our natural constitution but the fact that we have received the operating God. God is now operating in us.

Paul uses great words in the book of Philippians to speak of the experience of Christ. Paul says that he magnified Christ. To magnify is to show or declare great (without limitation), to exalt, and to extol. Paul speaks of the bountiful supply of the Spirit of Jesus Christ, and he says that for him to live is Christ. At the end of Philippians Paul says, "All the saints greet you, and especially those of Caesar's household" (4:22). Caesar's household comprised all who were attached to the palace of Nero. Some of these were converted through contact with Paul and became believers in Christ in Rome. No doubt, some in Caesar's household became Christians because they saw Christ in Paul. The majority, however, did not see Christ in Paul. Surely, Christ was with Paul all the time, but many did not see. Seeing Christ in such a way depends upon the Lord's mercy. It depends upon whether God has chosen and predestinated someone. Paul magnified Christ before everyone, but not everyone saw this magnification. This was because they did not receive the Lord's mercy. They were not chosen and predestinated. God's operating in us is not outwardly spectacular, but in a spiritual sense it is a great matter. If we have the spiritual discernment, the spiritual realizing power, we can see that all the things in the book of Philippians related to God's operating in us are great.

With the Bountiful Supply
of the Spirit of Jesus Christ

God's operating in us is with the bountiful supply of the

Spirit of Jesus Christ (1:19). In Philippians 1:19 Paul says, "I know that for me this will turn out to salvation through your petition and the bountiful supply of the Spirit of Jesus Christ." In Philippians 2:12 Paul charges us to work out our own salvation. On the one hand, the bountiful supply of the Spirit of Jesus Christ will turn out to be our salvation, and on the other hand, we have to work out our salvation. Philippians 1 and 2 refer to the same salvation. This salvation is the working out, the issue, of the bountiful supply of the Spirit of Jesus Christ, and this salvation is something that we work out in our living.

Martin Luther said that salvation is not by works but by faith. But Paul told us to work out our own salvation. We need to see that the very salvation revealed in the entire New Testament is an all-inclusive salvation. The salvation that Martin Luther referred to is justification. To be justified by God is to be forgiven of our sins so that we can be delivered from God's condemnation out of the lake of fire. This is God's salvation in justification. In Philippians Paul was speaking of a salvation that is continuing in our daily walk to save us from things such as selfish ambition (1:17), vainglory (2:3), murmurings, and reasonings (v. 14).

Murmurings come mostly from the sisters, and reasonings come mostly from the brothers. Have you been saved from murmurings and reasonings? We are saved to some extent but not fully. We need to be continuously saved until we enter into the New Jerusalem. In our marriage life we need to be saved from murmurings and reasonings. The husbands may reason, and the wives may murmur. Murmurings and reasonings are very small, but they are very troublesome. Both frustrate us from carrying out our salvation to the fullest extent, from experiencing and enjoying Christ to the uttermost.

If we look at salvation from this angle, we realize that we need to be saved continuously. Many years ago when people asked me if I had been saved, I would boldly tell them that I was saved. But today if you ask me the same question, I will ask you what you mean by my being saved. Have I been saved from the lake of fire? Surely, I have been saved from that, but there are still a number of things from which I need to be saved. In order to magnify Christ and live Christ, we need to be saved from murmurings and reasonings. To be saved from our murmurings and reasonings, we need the operating God. It is God who operates in us both the willing and the working for His good pleasure through the bountiful supply of the Spirit of Jesus Christ.

We need God's operating and the bountiful supply of the Spirit of Jesus Christ. The bountiful supply of the Spirit of Jesus Christ is "the bountiful groceries," and God's operating is "God's cooking." We need the groceries and the cooking of the groceries. Today God is operating within us miraculously yet normally. We should learn to cooperate with Him. Our cooperation is our obedience. This is why Paul says in Philippians 2:12, "Even as you have always obeyed, not as in my presence only but now much rather in my absence, work out your own salvation with fear and trembling." We should obey by cooperating with God's operating. As God operates, we need to obey.

For Us to Live Christ for His Magnification

The bountiful supply of the Spirit of Jesus Christ is for us to live Christ for His magnification (1:20-21a). We need to magnify Christ under any kind of circumstance. Philippians 1:20 says, "According to my earnest expectation and hope that in nothing I will be put to shame, but with all boldness, as always, even now Christ will be magnified in my body, whether through life or through death." Paul says that he was magnifying Christ, as always, through the bountiful supply of the Spirit of Jesus Christ. This is altogether under God's operating.

By Holding Forth the Word of Life, as Luminaries Shining in This Age

We live Christ for His magnification by holding forth the word of life (2:15-16a). *To hold forth* is "to apply," "to present," or "to offer." To hold forth the word of life is to present the word of life to people as an offering, a contribution. Our Christian life is a life of holding forth the word of life to present it to others as an offering, a contribution. We hold forth the word of life as luminaries shining in this age (v. 15). As to our location, we are in the world; as to our condition, we are in this age. This age is corrupt, dark, evil, and perverted. But we are on this earth shining in this age as luminaries to reflect the divine light of Christ. A luminary does not have light in itself, but it reflects the light of the sun. We are luminaries who have no light in ourselves. We reflect the light of the sun, Christ. This is what it means to live Christ for His magnification. We hold forth the word of life as luminaries shining in this age.

To Work Out Our Salvation

Our holding forth the word of life is to work out our salvation, to carry out our salvation (v. 12). Paul tells us to work out our own salvation, and then he mentions that we need to do all things without murmurings and reasonings (v. 14). As we have pointed out, both murmurings and reasonings frustrate us from carrying out our salvation to the fullest extent. We need to carry out our salvation, to bring it to its ultimate conclusion, by our constant and absolute obedience with fear and trembling. We have received this salvation by faith, but now we must carry it out by obedience. To receive it by faith is once for all, whereas to carry it out is lifelong.

Gaining Christ and Being Found in Christ

In Philippians 2 God's operating is for us to work out our own salvation without murmurings and reasonings. For this we need to take Christ as our model, our pattern. In chapter 3 we see that we need to be those gaining Christ and being found in Christ (vv. 8-9). The real gain is Christ. Anything other than Christ is a loss. In Philippians 3:7-8 Paul says, "What things were gains to me, these I have counted as loss on account of Christ. But moreover I also count all things to be loss on account of the excellency of the knowledge of Christ Jesus my Lord, on account of whom I have suffered the loss of all things and count them as refuse that I may gain Christ."

To gain Christ may be compared to gaining the victory in a war. To gain the victory in a war, everything has to be sacrificed. When the United States declared war in World War II, the entire country with all its citizens sacrificed everything to gain the victory in the war. Without that kind of sacrifice the United States could not have helped to win World War II. Today we also need to sacrifice everything to gain Christ. We need to tell Satan that we are going to fight to win the victory to gain Christ.

We also need to be found in Christ. Everyone should be able to see that we are persons in Christ. When Paul was Saul of Tarsus, he was absolutely in the law. When people found him, saw him, he was a person in the law. But in Philippians 3 Paul declares that he wanted only to be found in Christ; he was only for Christ, and he wanted to be found by everyone in Christ. Paul was a man in Christ (2 Cor. 12:2a).

By Knowing Christ as Our All
and by Knowing the Power of His Resurrection
to Be Conformed to His Death

We gain Christ and are found in Christ by knowing Christ as our all and by knowing the power of His resurrection to be conformed to His death (Phil. 3:10). Paul indicates in Philippians 3 that he was a person pursuing Christ (vv. 12, 14). The Greek word for *pursue* is the same word for *persecute*. Paul did two kinds of persecuting. The first kind of persecuting was a negative kind of persecuting. Paul persecuted Christ in this way when he was Saul of Tarsus. But after he was saved, he began to persecute Christ in a positive sense. To persecute Christ in a positive way is to press toward Christ, to follow after Christ. Paul realized that in order to pursue Christ, to persecute Christ, he needed the power of Christ's resurrection, a power that can overcome death, subdue death, defeat death, and bring us out of death's usurpation.

Paul aspired to know Christ and the power of His resurrection so that he could be conformed to Christ's death. A. B. Simpson says, "'Tis not hard to die with Christ / When His risen life we know" (*Hymns,* #481). When we have resurrection as our enjoyment, this enjoyment enables us to be conformed to the death of Christ. Christ's death is a model, a mold, and we are like pieces of dough that are put into this mold so that we can be conformed to the image of this mold. The mold that we are being conformed to is the death of Christ.

Each one of us has a certain amount of problems and sufferings. We may have sufferings related to our health, our finances, or our children. Who has no suffering? No one is in a situation in which everything is complete, perfect, satisfactory, fine, and in the third heaven. Who has a perfect, complete, satisfactory, and heavenly marriage? There is not such a marriage on this earth. Even marriage can be a real suffering. No one can escape suffering. These sufferings should be a mold. After we have been saved, God's sovereignty puts us into this mold. This is the mold of the death of Christ. We need the power of resurrection to be conformed to the death of Christ. We need to be in the image of Christ and also in the image of His death. For this we need the power of His resurrection, not our natural power.

To Obtain the Out-resurrection
from among the Dead as Our Reward

We want to be those who know Christ and the power of His resurrection to be conformed to His death so that we can obtain the out-resurrection from the dead as our reward (vv. 11-14). In Greek the word for *resurrection* in Philippians 3:11 has the prefix *ex* before it. *Ex* means "extra." This resurrection is the outstanding resurrection, the extra-resurrection, which will be a prize to the overcoming saints. This particular resurrection will be a great reward to us. We cannot reach or obtain this out-resurrection without the power of Christ's resurrection to conform us to the mold of His death.

Manifesting Forbearance
and Expressing the Virtue and Praise of God
in Whatever Is True, Dignified, Righteous,
Pure, Lovely, and Well Spoken Of

When we live with the Divine Trinity according to what is revealed of God operating in us in Philippians, we manifest forbearance and express the virtue and praise of God in whatever is true, dignified, righteous, pure, lovely, and well spoken of (4:5, 8). In Philippians 4:5 Paul says, "Let your forbearance be known to all men." This is to manifest forbearance. We saw in chapter 11 that the significance of the word *forbearance* is to be humble, to give in, to fit in any kind of situation, and to be able to be with any kind of person under any kind of circumstance. Forbearance implies humility, meekness, endurance, and patience. We need to let this virtue of forbearance be known to others, and this is to manifest the forbearance of Christ. In 2 Corinthians 10:1 Paul entreats the saints through the meekness and gentleness, or forbearance, of Christ. This is the forbearance of Christ that Paul lived and mentions in Philippians 4. We also need to express the virtue and praise of God in whatever is true, dignified, righteous, pure, lovely, and well spoken of. These virtues are the expression of a person who is living Christ for Christ's magnification. When Christ is magnified, these virtues will be expressed. Then there will be praise to God.

By the Secret in Taking Christ
as Our Satisfaction

We manifest forbearance and express the virtue and praise of God by the secret in taking Christ as our satisfaction (v. 12). We mentioned that "the secret" indicates being ushered into a secret society. Paul uses this to illustrate that we Christians are ushered into a particular society, and this particular society is the church, the Body of Christ. In this secret society Christ is the secret whom we need to learn for our initiation. We must take Christ as our secret so that we can enjoy Him all the time as our satisfaction.

Being Strengthened in Christ for All Things

Eventually, we will be strengthened in Christ, in the One who empowers us to do all things (v. 13). Christ empowers us, makes us dynamic from within, not from without. By such an inward empowering, Paul could do all things in Christ. Thank the Lord for the revelation of living with the Divine Trinity in the book of Philippians!

CHAPTER THIRTEEN

LIVING WITH THE DIVINE TRINITY

(4)

Scripture Reading: Matt. 28:19; 2 Cor. 13:14; Jude 20-21; Rev. 1:4-5; John 17:22-23; Rev. 21:22-23; 22:1-5

Our fellowship in this chapter may be considered as covering the concluding section of the entire revelation concerning the Divine Trinity in both the New Testament and the Old Testament.

ENJOYING THE DIVINE TRINITY IN FULL

Having Been Baptized into the Name (the Person) of the Father, the Son, and the Holy Spirit

At the conclusion of the Gospel of Matthew, the gospel of the kingdom, the Lord revealed that we have been baptized into the name [the person] of the Father, the Son, and the Holy Spirit (28:19). M. R. Vincent says that the word *into* in Matthew 28:19 indicates that baptism brings us into a spiritual and mystical union with the Triune God. The name of the Father, the Son, and the Holy Spirit in this verse is the sum total of the Divine Being, equivalent to His person. To baptize people into the name of the Triune God is to bring them into the person of the Triune God that they may have an organic union with this divine person. Our organic union with the Triune God brings us into a deep enjoyment and a rich experience of the Triune God. We were baptized into the Triune God so that we could experience Him and enjoy Him.

At the end of the New Testament in Revelation 22, a marvelous picture is presented, revealing the Triune God for our enjoyment. A river is flowing out of the throne, and a tree is growing along the two sides of the river (vv. 1-2). This tree is the tree of life yielding its fruit every month. In Revelation 2:7 the Lord Jesus said that He would give those who overcome to eat of the tree of life. The tree of life is first mentioned in Genesis 2. God's desire in Genesis 2 was for man to eat the tree of life, but man fell by eating the tree of the knowledge of good and evil. Sin entered into man, and man became flesh. Because of man's fall Genesis 3 records that God closed the tree of life to man, keeping man away by His righteousness, holiness, and glory (v. 24). Over four thousand years later Jesus came and accomplished redemption to fulfill God's requirements. Then the Lord declared in Revelation 2 that if we would overcome according to His will, He would give us to eat of the tree of life. The way to the tree of life has been opened again for all the redeemed ones who are willing to overcome according to the Lord's demand.

At the end of the Bible this tree of life is growing along the two sides of the river of water of life, which proceeds out of the throne of God. The tree of life signifies Christ as the very embodiment of the Triune God to be our food, our life supply. John 7:38 and 39 show clearly that the Spirit will be rivers of living water flowing out of our innermost being. Thus, the river of water of life is a symbol of the Spirit. I hope that we can see that the Trinity revealed in the Bible is not for doctrinal debate or for us to understand or study in a merely theological way. The very Trinity revealed in the Bible is altogether for our eating and drinking—for our enjoyment. We have been baptized into the Triune God who is to be our enjoyment, our food and our drink, that we may live by Him. Thus, we can say that Matthew 28:19 reveals to us the divine enjoyment, and our divine enjoyment is to feed on the Triune God and drink the Triune God. He is our tree of life and our river of water of life.

Participating in the Love of God, the Grace of Christ, and the Fellowship of the Holy Spirit

To enjoy the Divine Trinity in full is to participate in the love of God, the grace of Christ, and the fellowship of the Holy Spirit. Second Corinthians 13:14 says, "The grace of the Lord Jesus Christ and the love of God and the fellowship of the Holy

Spirit be with you all." Again, this verse shows that the Divine Trinity is not for the doctrinal study of theology but for our experience and enjoyment. The love of God the Father is the source, and the grace of Christ, God the Son, is the course of the love of God. When love comes out, it becomes grace. Then the fellowship of the Holy Spirit is the transmission, the communication, of the grace of Christ with the love of God the Father. Love is God the Father, grace as the outflow of love is Christ the Son, and the fellowship is the transmission of the Holy Spirit to transmit what the Son is as grace and what the Father is as love. The Holy Spirit transmits the divine riches into our being, and this transmission is the fellowship. Today we have the Divine Trinity operating in us in such a wonderful way.

In the previous chapter we saw the revelation of God operating in us. This operating of God is very quiet but very vigorous and efficient. Although electricity flows quietly, it is very vigorous and efficient. The current of electricity is the operating of the electricity. The love, grace, and fellowship moving within us form a kind of current within us. This current is the circulation of the Divine Trinity.

With the Divine Trinity are the source, the course, and the flow. The source, the fountain, of this circulation is the love of the Father. The course, the outflow, of this circulation is the very grace expressed and conveyed to us by Christ. The grace of Christ comes out of the source of the love of the Father. The flow is the Holy Spirit as the fellowship, the communication, the transmission, the circulation, of the grace of Christ with the love of the Father.

We have two circulations within us. One circulation is the circulation of blood within our physical body, and the other circulation is the circulation of the Divine Trinity in our spirit. Without either of these circulations we would die either physically or spiritually. Second Corinthians 13:14 gives us a detailed description of this inner, spiritual circulation. This circulation is the supply in our Christian life and church life. This is similar to saying that the current of electricity is the supply of power to an entire city. All the big cities on the earth today depend upon electricity. A number of years ago the current of electricity to the city of New York was cut off for a period of time. When that happened, the entire life of the city stopped. This is a very good illustration. We must see that the entire church life depends upon 2 Corinthians 13:14. It depends upon the love of the Father, the grace of the Son, and the fellowship of the Spirit to flow as a current within our spirit.

Many times while I am speaking in the ministry of the word, I have the inner sensation that the divine current is going on. If the current within me stops, I have nothing to speak. If we miss the Spirit in our speaking, our speaking is empty. Furthermore, if the current within us is cut off while we are listening to the ministry of the word, our listening is empty. We need to speak in the flow and listen in the flow. The flow is the transmission of the Holy Spirit, and this transmission is the fellowship that conveys the grace of Christ the Son as the outflow of the love of the Triune God. The current of the Divine Trinity within us as revealed in 2 Corinthians 13:14 is our spiritual pulse.

Praying in the Holy Spirit, Keeping Ourselves in the Love of God, and Awaiting the Mercy of Our Lord Jesus Christ unto Eternal Life

In Jude's concluding word of his Epistle, he charges us to pray in the Holy Spirit and keep ourselves in the love of God, awaiting the mercy of our Lord Jesus Christ unto eternal life (vv. 20-21). Jude is not teaching us theology, but he is charging us to enjoy the Divine Trinity. To enjoy the Divine Trinity, we need to pray. To pray is to get into the current of the Divine Trinity, to get into the fellowship of the Holy Spirit. Through this fellowship we reach the source of the love of God. Then in the love of God we await and look for the mercy of our Lord so that we may not only enjoy eternal life in this age but also inherit it for eternity (Matt. 19:29). In the opening of his Epistle, Jude mentions mercy (v. 2). Mercy is mentioned instead of grace due to the church's degradation and apostasy. We all need the Lord's mercy. This mercy is a bridge to the grace of Christ. We need to pray in the Holy Spirit that we may touch the source, the love of God, in which we await the mercy of our Lord Jesus Christ. This is the enjoyment of the Triune God.

To Be Consummated with Grace and Peace by the Father, Who Is, Who Was, and Who Is Coming, by the Seven Spirits, and by Jesus Christ, the Faithful Witness, the Firstborn of the Dead, and the Ruler of the Kings of the Earth

Our enjoyment of the Divine Trinity in full is consummated with grace and peace by the Father, who is, who was, and who is coming; by the seven Spirits; and by Jesus Christ, the faithful Witness, the Firstborn of the dead, and the Ruler of the kings of the earth (Rev. 1:4-5). Grace is the Triune God as our enjoyment, and peace is the issue, the result, of our enjoyment of grace. The more we enjoy the Triune God as our grace, the more we have peace within. In Revelation 1 the Father is referred to as the One who is, who was, and who is coming. As God the eternal Father, He was in the past, He is in the present, and He is coming in the future. This shows that even the Father Himself is triune. He is triune as the One who is, who was, and who is coming. The seven Spirits are the sevenfold intensified Spirit. The one Spirit has been intensified sevenfold. The sevenfold Spirit may be likened to a seven-way lamp. Such a seven-way lamp gives us the strongest light, the intensification of light. The Spirit today is intensified sevenfold because of the dark age.

According to Revelation 5:6, the seven Spirits of God are the seven eyes of Christ, the Lamb of God. Some theologians teach that the Son is separate from the Spirit, but in Revelation we see that the Spirit, the third of the Trinity, is the eyes of the Son, the second of the Trinity. A person's eyes are not separate from him. It is wrong to say that the second, the Son, is separate from the third, the Spirit. The Bible shows us that the third is the eyes of the second. Our eyes cannot be another person that is separate from us. This shows us the outwardness of the traditional teaching concerning the Trinity. Some have accused us of mixing up the three persons of the Godhead. Actually, it is the Bible that tells us that Christ is the Spirit (2 Cor. 3:17; 1 Cor. 15:45b). Furthermore, according to Revelation, the Spirit is the eyes of Jesus, the Son. The Divine Trinity is a wonderful mystery. Martin Luther said that anyone who could explain the Divine Trinity must be the teacher of God. The Son and the Spirit are two, yet They are one. How do we know that They are one? The strongest proof is that the third is the eyes of the second.

We may not be able to understand the Divine Trinity, but we can enjoy Him. Every day we eat and enjoy food that we do not know how to define. We do not understand the food, but we can enjoy the food. I do not know what is in an orange, but I can enjoy the orange by eating it. We may not understand what is in a glass of orange juice, but we can enjoy it as our refreshment. A person may take many vitamins without being clear what the vitamins do and what they are for. However, because he takes these vitamins into him, he receives the benefit of each vitamin. This is why I say that we need to learn to enjoy the Father, enjoy the Son, and enjoy the Spirit. When we pray, call on the name of the Lord, and get into the Word, we enjoy the Triune God as our divine vitamins. The Father may be likened to vitamin A, the Son to vitamin B, and the Spirit to vitamin C. We may not understand what these "vitamins" do for us, but we must learn to enjoy them. We may not fully understand the Triune God, but we must learn to enjoy Him, to receive the full benefit of all His riches. Matthew 28:19, 2 Corinthians 13:14, Jude 20-21, and Revelation 1:4-5 reveal to us the enjoyment of the Triune God. We need to be those who enjoy the Divine Trinity in full.

THE ISSUE OF OUR ENJOYMENT
OF THE DIVINE TRINITY

The issue of our enjoyment of the Divine Trinity is the oneness. In the previous chapters we have seen something of the excellent oneness among the three of the Godhead. As we look at the Divine Trinity, we see the revelation of the excellent oneness of the Godhead. The three always work together and act as one. Not one of the three ever acts independently. When one is there, the others are there also. The three of the Godhead are one. We can see the oneness of the Godhead in the Lord's prayer in John 17. No one can explain, define, or expound this prayer to the uttermost. How profound this prayer is! This prayer reveals that the issue of our enjoyment of the Divine Trinity is that we are brought into the divine oneness, and we become the copy, the reproduction, of the oneness among the three of the Trinity.

The oneness revealed in the Lord's prayer in John 17 is threefold. First, there is the oneness in the Father's name by the eternal life (vv. 6-13). Second, there is the oneness in the Triune God through sanctification by the holy word (vv. 14-21). Third, there is the oneness in the divine glory for the expression of the Triune God (vv. 22-24). The oneness by the glory, the expressed Divine Trinity, is the oneness among the three of the Divine Trinity. The glory that has been given to us is the very Triune God expressed. By this expression we are one, and our oneness is a reproduction of the oneness of the Triune God. This is why the Lord prayed, "The glory which You have given Me I have given to them, that they may be one, even as We are one" (v. 22). Then the Son prayed that we would be perfected into one by having the Divine Trinity in us—by living with the Divine Trinity (v. 23). To be perfected into one is the unique result, the unique issue, of our enjoyment of the Triune God.

The most difficult thing among Christians is to keep the oneness. Even among us believers in the Lord's recovery, it is not so easy to keep the real oneness. How can we reproduce the divine oneness as the copy of the oneness among the three of the Godhead? There is no other way except by enjoying the Triune God. We need to enjoy Him to the extent that the three of the divine Godhead can be expressed. Then the oneness is among us. This reproduced oneness is the issue of our enjoyment of the Triune God. We enjoy the Triune God until He is expressed in us, and this expression is the very oneness that is a copy of the oneness among the three of the Divine Trinity. The enjoyment of the Triune God will have a result, an issue. This will issue in the divine oneness that is the very reproduction of the divine oneness among the three of the Divine Trinity.

Things that are outside the Trinity are the dividing and separating factors. In order to keep the oneness, we need to reject, renounce, and deny anything that we have that is outside of the Triune God. We should deny, renounce, and reject anything that is not the Triune God Himself. Anything other than the Triune God Himself can become a dividing factor. We are perfected into one by having the Divine Trinity in us. To have the Divine Trinity in us is to live with the Divine Trinity. The way to have the oneness, which is the Divine Trinity expressed, is to live with the Divine Trinity.

ENJOYING THE DIVINE TRINITY
TO THE FULLEST IN ETERNITY

Eventually, we will enjoy the Divine Trinity to the fullest in eternity (Rev. 22:1-5). Regardless of how much we are enjoying the Divine Trinity today, we are still not enjoying Him to the fullest extent. The fullest enjoyment of our wonderful Triune God will be in eternity in the new heaven and new earth.

In this enjoyment we will have God and the Lamb [the redeeming God in His trinity] as the temple for our dwelling (21:22-23). The temple is the dwelling place and the serving place of the priests of God. In eternity we all will be God's eternal priests, and God Himself will be our dwelling in whom we live and serve. The temple in Revelation 21 is not a material temple. The temple is a person. Verse 22 tells us that the temple is the Lord God the Almighty and the Lamb, the redeeming God. Verse 23 tells us that the lamp of the city is the Lamb, the person of Christ. Because of this revelation, we have the boldness to say that the holy city, the New Jerusalem, is not a material city but a person.

The holy city is a corporate person, and this corporate person is a couple—the processed Triune God married to the transformed tripartite man. This is the Spirit and the bride becoming one (22:17a). Divinity and humanity are married together, mingled together, to be one entity. The holy city is a corporate person—a great corporate God-man. The holy city as the tabernacle of God is for God to dwell in (21:2-3), and God and the Lamb as the temple are for us to dwell in. God is our temple, and we are His tabernacle. In the new heaven and new earth the New Jerusalem will be a mutual dwelling place for both God and man for eternity.

The throne of God [the Triune God] and of the Lamb [the redeeming Son] is the center of the holy city for the divine administration and the source of the divine enjoyment to us (22:1, 3). The throne of God and of the Lamb is for the divine administration. It is also the source of our divine, eternal enjoyment because the river with the tree of life comes out of the throne. We will drink the river of water of life [the Spirit] proceeding out of the throne (v. 1). We will also eat the tree of life [the life-giving Son] growing on the two sides of the river, yielding fruit each month (v. 2). The life-giving Son yields fruit each month for our life supply. Thus, we have the redeeming God as our dwelling place, the throne as the source of our enjoyment, the Spirit as our drink, and the life-giving Son as our food.

We will also have the Lord God [the Triune God] illumining us (v. 5a). This means that our God will be our lamp. We will have the name of the Triune God on our forehead (v. 4b). The fact that we bear His name declares that we are one with Him. In a training we may wear a badge to tell people who we are. In eternity we will have a "badge" on our forehead. That badge declares that we belong to the Triune God and that we are one with the Triune God. Praise the Lord that we will bear such a "badge" for eternity! For eternity we will be labeled with the Triune God.

We will also see the face of the Triune God (v. 4a). In eternity future, in the new heaven and new earth and in the New Jerusalem, we will see the face of our God. To see the face of the Triune God and to have His name on our forehead will be blessings to us in eternity. Furthermore, we will serve the Triune God as His priests (20:6; 22:3b) and reign to the ages of the ages as the kings of the Triune God (v. 5b). In eternity future all the preserved nations around the New Jerusalem will be the citizens (21:24-27), the people of God's eternal kingdom, but we will be the kings who reign forever and ever.

Through our study of the revelation concerning living in and with the Divine Trinity, we can see that the entire New Testament is composed with the Triune God as its structure. The last picture of the divine revelation in Revelation 21 and 22 shows that the Triune God is not for our mental understanding but for our enjoyment. He is our dwelling place, our drink, our food, and our light. To maintain life, we need a dwelling place, drink, food, and light. As long as we have these four necessities, we can have a proper living. We have a place in which to dwell, water to drink, food to eat, and light to enjoy. All of these are the

Triune God. The Triune God is our dwelling place, the Son is our food, the Spirit is our drink, and the redeeming God is our light. This describes the coming life in eternity, which we will enjoy to the fullest.

ABOUT THE AUTHOR

Witness Lee was born in 1905 in northern China and raised in a Christian family. At age 19 he was fully captured for Christ and immediately consecrated himself to preach the gospel for the rest of his life. Early in his service, he met Watchman Nee, a renowned preacher, teacher, and writer. Witness Lee labored together with Watchman Nee under his direction. In 1934 Watchman Nee entrusted Witness Lee with the responsibility for his publication operation, called the Shanghai Gospel Bookroom.

Prior to the Communist takeover in 1949, Witness Lee was sent by Watchman Nee and his other co-workers to Taiwan to ensure that the things delivered to them by the Lord would not be lost. Watchman Nee instructed Witness Lee to continue the former's publishing operation abroad as the Taiwan Gospel Bookroom, which has been publicly recognized as the publisher of Watchman Nee's works outside China. Witness Lee's work in Taiwan manifested the Lord's abundant blessing. From a mere 350 believers, newly fled from the mainland, the churches in Taiwan grew to 20,000 in five years.

In 1962 Witness Lee felt led of the Lord to come to the United States, and he began to minister in Los Angeles. During his 35 years of service in the U.S., he ministered in weekly meetings and weekend conferences, delivering several thousand spoken messages. Much of his speaking has since been published as over 400 titles. Many of these have been translated into over fourteen languages. He gave his last public conference in February 1997 at the age of 91.

He leaves behind a prolific presentation of the truth in the Bible. His major work, *Life-study of the Bible,* comprises over 25,000 pages of commentary on every book of the Bible from the perspective of the believers' enjoyment and experience of God's divine life in Christ through the Holy Spirit. Witness Lee was the chief editor of a new translation of the New Testament into Chinese called the Recovery Version and directed the translation of the same into English. The Recovery Version also appears in a number of other languages. He provided an extensive body of footnotes, outlines, and spiritual cross references. A radio broadcast of his messages can be heard on Christian radio stations in the United States. In 1965 Witness Lee founded Living Stream Ministry, a non-profit corporation, located in Anaheim, California, which officially presents his and Watchman Nee's ministry.

Witness Lee's ministry emphasizes the experience of Christ as life and the practical oneness of the believers as the Body of Christ. Stressing the importance of attending to both these matters, he led the churches under his care to grow in Christian life and function. He was unbending in his conviction that God's goal is not narrow sectarianism but the Body of Christ. In time, believers began to meet simply as the church in their localities in response to this conviction. In recent years a number of new churches have been raised up in Russia and in many European countries.